What People Are Saying ...

"*ManQuest* took my relationships with my two sons to an entirely new place. Never would have done it on my own. The MQ curriculum is straightforward and easy to apply — it's plug-and-play for any adult man and teenage boy. Just do it!"

— Drew Y.

"A game changer for me and my son. As a coach, most of my time is spent on the court pouring into young men. I'm constantly seeking out resources to help raise my sons (and players) into happy, healthy young men of character. MQ sparked conversations and dialogue with my son that would have never happened in daily life. We went much deeper than I expected and it put a stake in the ground for a lifetime of meaningful discussions."

— Gary P.

"We all have good intentions to talk to our sons about 'man stuff,' but before we know it our sons are grown and we missed the moment. MQ takes the pressure off dads and gives them the tools to guide them through this transition. It will have a lifelong impact ... for both of us!"

— Jim T.

"MQ strengthened my relationship with each of my four sons and each time it rocked my world and took me to a new place. As you're talking to your son about the journey to manhood, you can't help but take a hard look in the mirror and ask yourself the same questions: What's my concept of manhood? Am I choosing to live as a man? With all four of my boys, MQ deepened my own journey."

— Mike R.

"If you're reading this, you're exactly the 'father' or 'father figure' who should take this leap of faith. You are clearly searching for something (or have heard something) that brought you to *ManQuest*. Respond to that 'nudge' and enjoy the ride with your son."

— Scott A.

"My teenage son doesn't get excited about much. But I was amazed at how much he wanted to better understand me and my story. *ManQuest* helped us peel back the onion and go to new places that deepened our relationship."

— Mark H.

"My son and I did MQ a couple of years ago and we still talk over the Guideposts and the discussion questions. In fact, we were so inspired by the experience, we created a family card game called 'Brave' to spark meaningful discussion and dialogue during family time. MQ inspired me to get off my butt and use my gifts to benefit others!"

— Calum M.

"My son had to deal with divorce in our family. His dad was unwilling to take him on a MQ journey, so I did the next best thing as a single mom — invited his grandfathers and uncles to speak into his life through MQ. My teenage daughter and I also use it to better understand the masculine psyche."

— Lynn S.

"MQ was so powerful for my son and me that I decided to share it with my old college fraternity buddies. For 5 straight weeks, 13 of us Skyped in and talked through the Guideposts and what it means to live as an adult man. Took our relationships to a whole new stratosphere."

— Greg M.

"My dad raised me to be 'tough guy.' Deep down I knew it was a faulty paradigm for manhood, but nobody ever taught me a different way. As I took each one of my three sons through *ManQuest*, I learned what real masculine strength looks like. Thanks to MQ, my boys have everything they need for the journey to manhood and I am forever changed."

— Jim N.

"*ManQuest* will take you and your son out of your comfort zone. MQ creates the environment to show him the real you. If your son sees you didn't 'magically' get to manhood unscathed, your honesty and vulnerability will earn trust and respect. He will bring you into his life and may even pour his heart out. A year after MQ, my son continues to open up to me; he's no longer afraid to broach any subject. You'll lay the foundation for something very special."

— Bradley F.

"As moms, we pour our heart and soul into raising our boys. But we only have so much to offer on the topic of being a man. They need their dad (or other man) to step up and guide them. Not easy for any mom to take a backseat with their son. But 10 years later, my sons are wonderful men and I directly attribute it to the *ManQuest* experience they shared with their dad."

— Sarah P.

"*ManQuest* was a great experience for my father and me a few years back. The challenges are bigger now that I'm in high school, but I'm confident in who I am — and the man I'm growing into."

— Hayden S.

What the Experts are Saying...

"Most of us want to teach our boys about authentic manhood but we don't always know what to say or where to start. *ManQuest* is the perfect guide for fathers and mentors who want to equip their teenage boys with the right stuff and start them on the adventure of a lifetime."

— Dave Dombrowski, General Manager, Boston Red Sox

"It goes without saying that boys need their fathers (and other adult men) to provide coming-of-age practices to catalyze and aid them in becoming men. *ManQuest* is a useful guide for any father who wants to take their young teenage sons on a 'rite of passage' journey."

— Ted Braude, Author, *How Boys Become Men*

"Finally, a playbook for coaching boys on what it takes to be a man. *ManQuest* delivers a healthy set of Guideposts to jumpstart teens on the road to manhood. Boys who never become men do a lot of damage; this book helps fathers teach boys a clear and compelling definition of manhood."

— Joe Ehrmann, NFL Legend, Pastor, Coach

MANQUEST:
Launching Teenage Boys Into Manhood

Mike McCormick

Edited by Karl Nilsson

For information on ordering bulk quantities of this book or to contact Mike McCormick for speaking engagements, address inquires to *ManQuestMovement@gmail.com.*

Stay connected at *www.ManQuestMovement.com*

MANQUEST:
Launching Teenage Boys into Manhood

To my sons, Xavier and Chase:

I'm proud of the men you are becoming! You have so much light to bring to this world. My greatest desire for you is not success or even happiness, but that you'll be open and available to the blessings that come your way. I hope you'll achieve great things, but let your accomplishments flow out of your giftedness and goodness — then you can have peace regardless of outcome. Thanks for teaching me and stretching me in new ways as a father and as a man. It's pure joy being your dad.

To my fellow men:

We are a band of wounded warriors. We live in silence with a nagging ache lurking just below the surface. It's something we can't quite place our finger on ... but we know it's there. No matter how attentive our dads may have been, we missed out on something deep and profound and life-giving.

And it affects everything we think, say and do.

Odds are, you're reading this book because you want things to be different for your son. I admire your strength and courage. At the end of this journey, the boy you share *ManQuest* with will realize beyond a shadow of a doubt that he is known, that he is loved, and that he is admired by an adult man. And this my friends, is the greatest blessing any man can ever give or receive.

MANQUEST

TABLE OF CONTENTS

SECTION 1: PASSING THE TORCH

MANQUEST

SECTION 2: THE ROADMAP

Foreword:
The Big Question

It was 3 a.m. on a hot summer night. I couldn't sleep. I tried to relax my mind and slip into dreamland, but I just couldn't. We had a big day coming up and a long drive ahead of us, but I couldn't find the rest I desperately needed.

In the next few hours — after 18 years of "all-in" fathering — I would be taking my son, Xavier, off to college and releasing him into the world.

Looking back, the arrival of that little guy changed my life in a profound way. There's nothing like the birth of a child to give crystal clarity to your meaning and purpose in life. The first time I saw him I was bowled over by a tidal wave of protectiveness and responsibility I'd never known. I remember taking him home from the hospital and feeling like the staff must have violated some child endangerment law by letting us leave with him. I didn't know what I was doing and there was no owner's manual to consult. I felt completely out of control.

As I tossed and turned on the eve of our big drop-off, those same feelings of protectiveness, responsibility and lack of control overwhelmed me again. But there was one big difference that made the "drop-off" even *more* emotional than his birth — I now had 18 years of love and memories invested in our relationship. All of my fathering instincts to protect and support were shifting toward something brand new, something called "letting go."

There are a few seminal moments in the life of a dad, times when you can't help but pause, reflect and ask yourself the big question: "What kind of dad am I?" Most of the time we're too busy and distracted to even ask. But dropping your kid off at college makes you wonder if they are ready and how well you did in preparing them for life.

More tossing. More turning. I finally got out of bed and headed downstairs for a change of scenery to quiet my mind. Unexpectedly, I heard voices out on the front porch. I opened the door and found my two sons hanging out, reminiscing and saying their final goodbyes. I joined them and we spent another hour chatting and laughing (and crying). It was one of the best times the three of us ever shared together. Xavier was going to be fine. I was going to be fine.

But I still had some regrets. Like many fathers and sons, we didn't always see eye to eye during his high school years. He pushed the boundaries and I reeled him back in. It left some damage and scars in our relationship. And I wondered whether those "battles" were all worth it: *Was I too hard on him? Was I too lenient? Did I give him what he needed?*

As we said our final goodbyes outside his dorm room, my son surprised me with the gift of a lifetime. Xavier told me he had left a "special something" in my sock drawer at home — my Father's Day gift. It was a few months late, but I already knew what it was. Every year when the kids ask me what I want for Father's Day, I always reply, "Write me a card or letter." I don't need any more ties, golf balls, or Starbucks gift cards, so I ask them for a gift from their hearts.

When they were little, they'd simply write me an "*I-love-you-because …*" card. During their teen years, they blew off the request altogether or bought me a token present. This time, I was pretty confident I was going to get a letter from my son!

The trip home from New York City was exhausting. My 7-year-old daughter sobbed for three hours straight with varying spurts of hysteria. My wife was somber and reflective (she had cried the entire way to New York). My 15-year-old son was pumped to get back home and take over his brother's bigger room. My mood? After months of anxiety, I was finally at peace. I was confident he was in the right place. But most of all, I was excited to get home and read my letter. I remember having the same feeling I get when it's time for my annual performance appraisal at work — overall, I'm pretty confident, but heck, you never know. As a dad, real and raw feedback from the kids is pretty rare. I was preparing myself to receive some.

When the car pulled into the driveway around midnight, I raced upstairs and found a quiet place to read the letter. It was the gift of a lifetime. It was heartfelt and affirming. He told me things I never knew — things I longed to hear. Basically, he let me know that he wouldn't change a thing about his childhood and our relationship. Even through the challenging times, he said he never doubted my love and support. He specifically referenced his *ManQuest* experience and thanked me for my guiding hand in his life. He was excited about his next step and felt well-equipped for life.

When it comes to raising kids — especially in today's world — you're never quite sure if your best is going to be good enough. This business of fathering is tough, full of dangers, pitfalls, and potential disasters. Rarely does it ever work out the way you planned.

That's why it's so important to seize this moment. It'll be over in the blink of an eye. Trust me. Your son will be graduating from high school before you know it. Do something epic for him, right now! Don't wait. Give him something he absolutely needs and secretly craves — the roadmap to manhood. The gift you give him now will strengthen and guide him long after you're gone.

It will be a lasting legacy that will bless future generations of your family.

But here's the catch — he'll never ask you for it. You need to initiate the whole thing. Don't ask him whether he "wants" to do *ManQuest*. Just tell him it's an important gift you want to give to him. If he says he doesn't want to do it, tell him it's not his choice. Ask him to simply trust you.

Gentlemen, *ManQuest* is not for the faint of heart. It has the potential to shift your entire masculine paradigm if you let it. This is not simply a check-the-box exercise. It will require you to dig a little deeper and go beyond your comfort zone.

Be bold and courageous. Don't let the voices in your head keep you from doing something your son desperately wants and needs. Sure, there are plenty of excuses to skip it — but don't! Get moving and give him what he needs most.

I can't guarantee your son will turn out exactly how you want him to.

But I *can* guarantee this — at the end of the *ManQuest* experience, you will feel closer to your son and he will know you did something heroic on his behalf! He may not remember everything he learned during *ManQuest*, but he will feel your love in action. By showing him the way and putting yourself out there, you will strengthen his resilience and help him step into the challenges of life with an extra jolt of confidence.

And that's the most important gift an adult man can ever give a teenage boy.

Recently, I dropped off my second son, Chase, at college in Los Angeles. It was a similar experience to Xavier's New York drop-off. Only this time, *I* was the one who wrote *him* a letter. I reminded him of the key takeaways from his *ManQuest* journey of five years ago. I reaffirmed that he has everything it takes to a be a great man in this world. And that I will be there to support him in every way possible.

> *He may not remember everything he learned during ManQuest, but he will feel your love in action."*
>
> – Mike McCormick

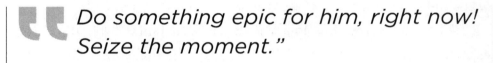

Do something epic for him, right now! Seize the moment."

— Mike McCormick

Introduction:
Setting a New Course

Would you ever give your car keys to a third-grader?

Recently, an eight-year-old Ohio boy hopped in his dad's work van and drove to McDonald's for a cheeseburger with his four-year-old sister riding shotgun. The boy raided his piggy bank to finance their craving for fast food and swiped the keys after his father went to bed early.

Miraculously, the child maintained the speed limit, stopped at four red lights, and executed a perfect left turn into the drive-thru. Apparently, he was able to reach the pedals by standing up while driving.

After getting multiple calls, police intercepted the pair at the drive-thru as they were placing their order. Officers said, "He looked up how to drive on YouTube."

No parent in their right mind would simply toss the car keys to a child and say, "Go figure it out on your own, you've got this." Yet that's exactly how we pass down the "keys of manhood" to teenage boys in America!

Fortunately, no one was hurt during the little boy's grand theft auto, but millions of young men *are* hurt when fathers fail to pass on wisdom for becoming a healthy man.

Most people agree that our society needs more men of character and principle. But we don't have an accepted process or agreed-upon set of customs to raise up the next generation of men with any intentionality. Our boys are flying blind out there with a lack of information and formal training. We sit idly by while advertisers tell them they can acquire manhood by spending lots of money on their products. We remain silent as our boys learn the ways of manhood from unreliable sources like Twitter, Snapchat, Spotify, Netflix, HBO and ESPN.

Ask 100 people what it means to "be a man," and you'll probably get 100 different answers. In today's world, people seem to have a clearer definition about what a man *isn't* rather than what a man should be.

We say (or think) things like: real men don't wear pink, real men don't wear yoga pants, real men don't drink chardonnay, don't take selfies, don't watch reality TV, don't _____(fill in the blank).

The list goes on and on. Most of us have pretty strong opinions on what makes a man, well, not a man. But we rarely shed any light on the essence of masculinity and how a man should conduct himself. As a result, there's a great deal of confusion about manhood and masculinity in our society — and we rarely pass along any meaningful information to the next generation.

Meanwhile, young men are starving for some reliable guidance and direction on what it means to be a man in this world. They are absolutely clueless and highly susceptible to the misguided masculine messages from the culture.

When my son Chase was in middle school, a boy on his basketball team walked outside into subzero cold after practice and took off his coat. He turned to his buddies and crowed, "Look at me, I'm a man." His teammates all laughed in agreement and removed their coats in a show of solidarity. They stood out there freezing together like Navy SEALs — thinking they were being manly by acting tough (and catching pneumonia)!

———

Are you a soccer dad, hockey dad, or football dad?

Today's father likely spends more time with his boys than previous generations. But are we really *engaged?* Are we transferring what they need to learn to become mature, healthy men? "Time spent" is definitely a good start, but it's not the best measuring stick for being a successful dad.

We may take him to a ballgame, drive him to his sports or even help with homework. But that's only a fraction of what boys really need from their dads. Rarely do we use our words to teach them, instruct them, and proactively guide them toward manhood. We can do a lot of the "right" things, but still not fully equip our boys for the journey to manhood. Boys need so much more from us than being a chauffeur, a cheerleader, or just another buddy.

So what's a dad to do? We need to fortify our boys with man skills *before* they get started on their manhood journey, so they don't get hopelessly lost. Sadly, many dads wait until *after* their son is stranded on the roadside of life before offering him a map or a GPS. And by that time, it might be too late.

Cultures across the globe actively initiate teenage boys into manhood with all sorts of rituals, customs, and practices. In America, we just expect our boys to figure it out on their own.

There's an incredible window of opportunity to equip our young men with all the tools they need for manhood. Between the ages of 12 and 14, young men are intensely curious when it comes to "man stuff."

Middle school is the perfect time to start the training, but they won't go there on their own.

Fathers need to actively move their boys from the La-Z-Boy to the launching pad of life.

The scary reality of upcoming life changes and responsibilities causes many boys to hit "pause" on the cusp of manhood. They are afraid of what lies ahead. Without active guidance from an adult man at this crucial time, many will get stuck in "Boyland" and resist the transition.

A lot of "man-boys" suffer from arrested development and never move beyond emotional adolescence. They spend their adult lives trying to recapture the comfort and security of their youth. These men live in a time warp — seeing the world through the eyes of a 13-year-old boy.

This is why the *active initiation* of teenage boys is imperative.

The window of opportunity to impart the wisdom of manhood to a teenage boy closes very quickly. **Most dads miss it altogether**. When a young man reaches high school, a "steel curtain" drops down and puts a seal on his concept of masculinity.

What he's learned up to that point is basically the playbook he'll use for the rest of his life.

Please read that again!

I'm not sure if it's due to girls, puberty, learning to drive, or whatever, but a man's core masculine psyche is usually defined around the time he reaches high school. If you miss this window, his concept of masculinity is pretty much locked in for the next 20 years or so, unless a major life event forces him to open it back up.

Don't believe me? Think about the guys you knew from middle school. Have they really matured that much over the years? While their physical features have changed, I'm guessing their outlook on life is pretty much the same as it was in the 8th grade.

————

The number of teenage boys getting sidetracked on the journey to manhood is just plain staggering. Think a man's influence isn't important to a boy? Over 70 percent of long-term prison inmates grew up in fatherless homes. Even "good" kids from "good" families in "good" neighborhoods are struggling to find their masculine footing.

What's the biggest problem in America? Drugs? Crime? I submit the number one issue in our society is that *teenage boys are not growing up into men.*

It affects everybody and everything.

My friend and mentor, Joe Ehrmann, says, "You can take any social issue — whether its girls with babies, boys with guns, or male violence toward women — and trace its roots back to some form of counterfeit masculinity. We have far too many little boys walking around in big boy bodies doing a lot of damage in our society because nobody ever taught them what a man should say and do in this world."

As a former NFL defensive lineman and coach, Ehrmann knows a thing or two about male behavior. He maintains that every young man needs a masculine foundation, something real, true, and specific to build his manhood on. If he never receives a reliable construct, society fills in the gaps with misinformation.

That's why the greatest gift a father can give his teenage son is the *ManQuest* roadmap to becoming a man. Manhood is *taught*, not *caught*. Men are *made* not *born*. You are responsible for shaping your son's concept of masculinity. Don't pass it off to his teacher, coach, camp counselor, tutor, Boy Scout leader, etc. Invite them to help out, but it's up to you to lead the way.

I recently heard about a guy who hired a police detective to teach his son how to be a man. I guess he didn't feel like he had the traditional masculine interests and hobbies to impart to his son. While I admire his initiative and care for his son's journey to manhood, the father didn't have to hire a stand-in. In reality, he was fully equipped to give his son everything he needed.

What about men *without* teenage sons? You are not off the hook! Just about every adult male has a teenage boy in his life — a brother, step-son, nephew, grandchild, player, student, neighbor, etc. to pour into.

Adult men have been abdicating our responsibility to train up the next generation with a healthy view of masculinity for too long.

It's time we set a new course.

One of the pastors at my church recently shared that when he was four years old, his dad died of cancer. He explained how living without a father figure left him confused and vulnerable. During middle school, he was severely bullied. He hated class. He dreaded going. He even contemplated suicide. Looking back, he felt that if his dad had been there, he'd have shown him how to navigate the bullying, or at the least, stepped in to stop it. He confessed to feeling "helpless, hopeless, and worthless." Fortunately, a male mentor entered his life. An adult friend from his church drove 45 minutes every Friday to connect, teach, and pour into this young man. He gave this future pastor exactly what he needed at just the right time.

That's the power of a mentor!

––––––––

"This business of becoming a man is the Great Trial of every male's existence, played out over a lifetime." That's from Franciscan friar and author Richard Rohr. He warns, "Our perilous journey is all the more difficult because we live in a time with very few mentors willing to show us the way."

Most men have good intentions.

In general, dads *want* to prepare their sons for manhood, but they don't know where to start or what to say. That awkward "birds and the bees" talk just doesn't cut it anymore. Let's face it, the game has changed and we need an entirely new playbook to keep up with our boys. ManQuest is designed specifically to give adult men the tools they need to engage teenage boys in conversations about the journey to manhood. And if the adult man opens himself up to the experience, it can prove to be life-changing for him as well!

What about mothers?

ManQuest helps women better understand the men in their lives — both their husbands and their little boys (who they desperately want to see become great men). *ManQuest* is a useful tool for all parents — fathers *and* mothers — but it's designed specifically for dads to guide their sons on the journey.

Section 1 of the book lays the groundwork for healthy masculinity and why we must to pass the torch to the next generation. **Section 2** provides a step-by-step guide to engaging teenage boys in essential conversations about manhood.

What would happen if dads and adult men embraced their roles as mentors, and proactively taught every teenage boy the ways of manhood? There's no question we would significantly enhance the fabric of our families, communities, and society — one boy at a time.

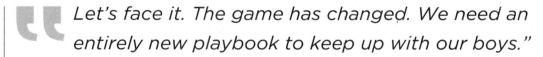

> *Let's face it. The game has changed. We need an entirely new playbook to keep up with our boys."*
>
> — Mike McCormick

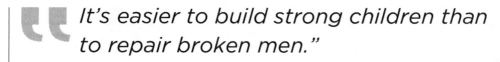 *It's easier to build strong children than to repair broken men."*

— Frederick Douglass, Abolitionist, Orator, Statesman

Section One:
Passing the Torch

> *Our story begins like so many stories — with a boy, too old to be a kid and too young to be a man."*
>
> — Introduction to the 2017 Disney Movie, *A Monster Calls*

A Force Awakens

Ancient mythologies, Hollywood blockbusters, and classical literature all tell the same familiar story: A wise guru comes alongside a young man to train him up and launch him on his journey to manhood. The plot is in three acts — at first the young man resists, then he struggles to learn his lessons from the master, and finally he's ready to be put to the test.

Why do we love these stories so much? Because every male has a secret yearning for an older man to notice him and shower him with time, attention, and wisdom. From *Karate Kid* to *Star Wars* to *Lord of the Rings*, the hero's journey captures the male heart.

The concept of initiation isn't new — it's been around forever.

Cultures across the globe have learned that the male, if left to his own devices, will become dangerous and even destructive to society. We see the consequences of that every day in some form or fashion.

In his book, *From Wild Man to Wise Man,* Richard Rohr says, "Young males don't naturally gravitate to building up the common good, but invariably pursue their own advancement or pleasure, regardless of consequences."

Rohr suggests, "Men have always needed a painful jolt, a fall from the proverbial tower, or a bloody reminder to become wise, contributing members of the larger community." In other words, they need a *launching pad* to thrust them toward manhood. Rohr adds, "Lacking a formal initiation process, modern America is not a healthy culture for boys. And that's largely because we lack wise elders who know how to pass on wisdom, identity, and boundaries."

Rohr maintains, "The general assumption underlying all initiation rites is that unless a young male is shown *real* power through a community of wise elders, he will seek *false* power. He will likely spend much of his life chasing the false gods of prestige, power, and possessions."

An old African proverb echoes this basic truth, "If you don't initiate your young men into manhood, they'll burn down the village just to feel the heat."

Since Colonial times, Americans have viewed our freedom and individuality with pride. Today, the concept of "doing our own thing" is still a badge of honor. We prize independent men and entrepreneurs who break the mold. But for most of recorded history, boys learned their *father's* trade and carried on the family business. In rural and urban environments, fathers and sons worked side by side — from the farm fields to the fishing boat to the blacksmith shop. While they worked, innumerable life lessons, impromptu discussions, and male bonding moments were shared.

That tradition is long gone.

According to Rohr, males in modern society are "over-mothered" and "under-fathered," especially when moms are forced to fill the gap left by physically or emotionally absent dads. Too many moms are being asked to play *both* parenting roles, which is a heavy burden they were never meant to carry. Don't get me wrong, mothers play a crucial role in the healthy development of young men. But unfortunately, mom is just about the last person a young man is going to come to for advice on manhood.

Teenage boys are looking for a guide whose already been on the journey he's preparing to embark upon. They long for someone to show them how to harness and unleash their masculine energy. While mom has plenty of wisdom to share on the topic of manhood, she's never walked the road he needs to travel. She can only take him so far.

There are countless coming-of-age stories, tales where a boy sets out on a journey toward manhood. Think Luke Skywalker, Tom Sawyer, and Frodo. Even Simba from *Lion King*. But in all the boys-to-men stories, I can't recall a single time when a boy asks his mom to show him the way.

Although it's not very politically correct to say, teenage boys need to find some independence apart from the safety and nurture of women — to activate their manhood within.

Here's the challenge: Many men have abdicated their roles as fathers. In over half the homes in America, there is no adult man present to teach, share, or inspire boys. And our society is feeling the effects of this leadership vacuum. The journey to manhood is *not* a solo trip. It must be initiated by an engaged father or male mentor.

Most people think Shakespeare's *Romeo and Juliet* is about tragic love. But in reality, it's a story of absentee fathers who provided no guidance or direction to their teenage sons who needed it desperately. "Low-impact fathering" is an issue that's been relevant since the dawn of time, and it's getting worse with every passing generation.

Sadly, most men don't have the words to teach boys about the journey to manhood. So they say and do nothing — and that scenario gets repeated over and over. For generations. It's hard to give something to your son that your father never gave to you. And very few of us ever received the gift of masculinity from *our* dad. As a result of our silence, young men in our society are grasping at straws, struggling to find their masculine soul.

————

In the *Star Wars* movie, *The Force Awakens*, there's a scene that captures the angst and uncertainty teenage boys experience while trying to grow into men. During the climax of the movie, Han Solo is standing on a catwalk in a space station with his estranged son Ben. Han is trying to coax his son away from the dark side and toward renewing their father-son relationship. Han tells Ben to take off the mask he's been wearing — the symbol of false power and strength he is hiding behind.

The father tells his son, "You don't need it anymore." When Ben removes his mask, Han passionately celebrates, "My son is alive!" Then, in a moment of confusion and honesty, Ben tells his dad, "I want to be free of this pain. I know what I have to do, but I don't know if I have the strength to do it. Will you help me?"

His father Han responds by pledging, "Yes, anything."

This is the perfect metaphor for the father-son relationship. Our young men are standing on the precipice of life and need an adult man to reach out their hand and show them the ropes. They are in quiet agony and hiding behind a mask they've created to convince the world that they have it all together. But behind the façade, they are scared little boys without the strength, or even the knowledge, to do what they need to do.

Ben asks his dad for something teenage boys rarely ask their fathers for — *help*. Is that because our boys are conditioned to never show weakness? Are they worried we won't give them the answers they need? Do they wonder if we even know the answers?

It's symbolic and worth noting that after opening up to his dad and exposing his needs and weaknesses, Ben gets scared and retracts. He misuses his light saber (a symbol of power) to kill Han. It's a shocking, unforgettable scene. Like Ben, many teenage boys are confused and hopeless and picking up instruments of false strength and power — using them to inflict damage on society and others. Not because they are malicious or evil, but because nobody ever showed them how to harness the force within.

―――――

"Teens age 13 to 18 spend almost nine hours a day on 'entertainment media' —including social media, music, gaming, and online videos." That's according to Common Sense Media, a nonprofit that tracks how kids use technology. The study, published in *USA Today*, shows tweens aged 10 to 12 are close behind, consuming six hours per day. Add in traditional TV viewing and the number's even higher.

Although it's tough to accept, your son's concept of masculinity is being shaped by Madison Avenue, Hollywood, Silicon Valley and the music industry. Right in front of your eyes!

It's no wonder we need a whole new language for explaining masculinity — one that connects with the hearts and minds of a media-saturated generation. Our boys are crying out for somebody to make sense out of all the chaos and conflicting voices swirling around them. Competing messages from the internet, video games, and movies embed false masculine stereotypes in their brains from a young age.

Today's media-savvy, high-tech boys need to realize there are still such things as true strength, noble virtue, and values worth fighting for. They need to know that living with open hearts and open hands doesn't make them soft or weak, but strengthens them. They may never admit it, but they long for a firm foundation and something (or someone) to believe in.

Who will provide them what they need — Google? Snapchat? Instagram?

Or you?

A Bad Hangover

A while back, a movie called *The Hangover* hit the big screen and spawned two sequels that earned almost a billion dollars worldwide. Bradley Cooper has moved on to bigger and better things these days, but *The Hangover* remains a classic buddy flick in our culture.

I've never seen any of the movies, but the first installment back in 2009 was a major reason I decided to write this book. Basically, *The Hangover* is about four friends who go to Las Vegas to celebrate a buddy's bachelor party with a weekend of boozing, gambling, strippers, and drugs. How do I know this? Because my son, Xavier, told me about it when he was twelve years old!

Before you get the wrong impression, let me stress that he didn't see the movie either. But sadly, most of his middle school buddies *did*. And they gleefully and graphically recounted all of the rip-roaring antics and sexual debaucheries to him.

Intrigued by the plot, my oldest son actually had enough nerve to ask if we could rent *The Hangover* for family movie night! I must say, the sheer audacity of his R-rated suggestion threw me for a loop. After all, we had only recently loosened the reins on PG-13. My first question was, "Did you get hit in the head during lacrosse?" After composing myself, I asked, "Since when did you turn 18?"

Predictably, he moaned about how all his friends had seen it, that he was the only kid in class who hadn't, and how I was the meanest, strictest dad, blah, blah, blah. Then he asked if I had any other lame reasons why he couldn't see it. "Absolutely," I replied. "I don't want you growing up thinking that sex, drugs, and rock-and-roll are what defines a man."

During our conversation, I flashed back to my early twenties, when I had my own *Hangover* type experience in Vegas. At a time when I was utterly clueless and trying to figure out this manhood thing, I went down some pretty dark paths in Sin City. I must say, the notion of "the sins of the father being passed down to the son" hit me like a Mike Tyson left hook. I realized that if I didn't start proactively teaching my boys what it means to be a man, they'd be at the mercy of a culture that's peddling a steady diet of false masculinity.

My son's Hangover request caught me off guard. While I was standing there flat-footed, he was learning about manhood from his misinformed locker room buddies. Realizing I only had a few years left to make a new impact, I started *ManQuest*. At the time, I thought it would be easy coming up with a paradigm to explain manhood, but it proved to be extremely difficult. (Try it yourself. Take a moment and write down your definition of a man. Not so easy!)

Some guys think manhood is passed from one generation to the next genetically, like blue eyes or curly hair. Others think it's passed on via osmosis — again, without any active intervention required. Osmosis can transfer fluid between molecules, but it *cannot* transmit values or character or morality from one person to another!

Perhaps you're thinking, "My dad never taught *me* anything about manhood, and *I* figured it out on my own." If so, I challenge you to consider how your life journey could have been different if your father had marked out a pathway. Not to mention, the negative messages are so much stronger today than when we grew up! Media is far more pervasive and persuasive. Remaining silent on the topic of manhood is no longer an option for fathers.

Guys, this is not a time to beat around the bush. Manhood lessons will not hit home if they are subtle or ambiguous — they must be specific, unvarnished, and powerful to make an impact.

———

A couple of summers ago, my son Chase started driver's training. To get him ready to hit the road, I took him for a local test drive. I was amazed at how little he knew about the intricacies of safe driving — turn signals, windshield wipers, high beams, etc. Then I flashed back to my own first driving experience.

When I was around 15, my mom unexpectedly offered me the keys. Out of the blue, she parked the family car on an abandoned stretch of dirt road and announced that I was going to drive. My heart was racing. *Is this really happening?* Her only instructions were to put the car in "Drive" and go slowly. I pulled away. I was doing about 25 mph when I reached my first curve. As I approached the left-hander, I didn't brake at all. I jerked the wheel, making a ridiculously sharp turn in our green 1979 Duster. We fishtailed back and forth until I managed to get the car straightened out.

I have no idea how the car stayed on the road!

My visibly shaken mother demanded I pull over immediately. With tears (and fear) in her eyes, she asked why I didn't brake before rounding the curve. I answered, "Nobody ever told me you have to brake when making a turn." She replied, "Haven't you been watching us drive all these years?" Somehow, I hadn't made the "brake-turn" connection during my days of backseat spectating. When it comes to driving, we can only learn so much from passive observation.

Same thing is true for *fathering*. You think your kid is soaking in all the manhood lessons he needs, but I guarantee he's not making as many connections as you believe. As a dad, I've spent far too much of my time "osmosis fathering." I remain silent and expect my boys to just watch me and miraculously catch on.

Don't get me wrong, being a good role model is a crucial part of a dad's job. But our boys need more from us. They need *intentional* dads who will use their words, feelings, and life experiences to teach proactive lessons about authentic manhood.

A friend recently confided something to me that many men feel but never articulate: "I've always tended to blame my frustrations and failures on my dad for not talking, teaching, and counseling me more. I always felt like he didn't prepare me for life." Can you relate?

You can be a "super dad" — fully engaged, loving, and concerned — but if your young man doesn't have a clear-cut construct of manhood by the time he enters high school, he will be ill-equipped for the journey that lies ahead.

Remember, you don't need to have all the answers to start a manhood discussion. Any young man will appreciate your willingness to start him on the journey. He will be grateful that somebody went over the "rules of the road" before handing him the keys to his manhood.

———

If my father would have started manhood conversations during my teenage years, there's no question it would have improved the trajectory of my life. And I had a great dad. He was active in my life and a positive role model. He was a strong influence and provided a safe, stable environment for me. He came home for dinner every night. Coached my sports teams. Encouraged me to do well in school. He took me to church. He stood up for me and believed the best about me. He did his best to set me on a successful path in life.

Growing up in my family, basketball was the king of our household. My older brother Tim had a dream to play in the NBA from an early age, so we played a lot of backyard basketball. As a result of countless hours of practice, I received a Division One scholarship to play at Kent State University. Tim grew to become a seven-footer and went on to fulfill his dream by playing 10 years in the NBA!

True confession: Basketball was never my main passion in life — I did it mostly so my dad would be proud of me. I thought my success on the court would somehow win his affection and attention. It didn't work. While I knew my awards and accolades made my dad happy, it never really brought us closer together. Unfortunately, I spent a lot of my childhood chasing after something that turned out to be a misguided pathway toward finding his love.

During my early years I was a pretty good kid. I kept my nose clean, excelled in sports, and got good grades. But as I got older and had to deal with bigger choices and adult issues, I lacked a clear and compelling definition of manhood. Once I graduated college, career decisions, relationship issues and moral choices forced me into new situations I was unprepared to handle.

As cultural pressures increased, my foundation started to crumble. And I got lost. Today, it's not uncommon for 20-something men to hit the wall and get stuck in midstream without any understanding why. That's what happened to me.

According to the Pew Research Center, for the first time in modern history, young men between the ages of 18-34, are more likely to live with their parents than a romantic partner. The millions of 20-something males living in their parents' basement, working a dead-end job, and playing video games incessantly is an alarming trend. Unfortunately, it's becoming all too common.

The number one strategy for combatting "failure to launch" syndrome is teaching and training our boys about manhood when they are eager to learn — during middle school. Believe it or not, the seeds we plant during those early teenage years will give them what they need to face life's challenges with confidence and conviction.

The Wonder Years

 Growing up is never easy. You hold onto things that were; you wonder what's to come. I think we knew it was time to let go of what had been, and look ahead to what would be — other days, new days, days to come."

— Kevin Arnold (The Narrator), *The Wonder Years*

My all-time favorite sitcom is a show called *The Wonder Years*. It ran from 1988 to 1993 (all 115 episodes are on Netflix). It's the saga of a teenage boy growing up in the late Sixties during a time of immense cultural change. Kevin Arnold, the show's protagonist, chronicles the inner thoughts and feelings of a middle school boy finding his way in a turbulent world. When I was in college, *The Wonder Years* absolutely captivated me, and I've only recently figured out why.

The truth is, there's a middle school boy living somewhere inside every man.

For most of us, this boy lives pretty close to the surface, and directly impacts our daily actions and thoughts. (Most women already know this and openly joke about the juvenile men in their lives.) We walk around in big boy bodies doing our big boy things every day. However, if we're completely honest, we long for the world to be comfortable, safe and simple. We want things to work out the way we want them to with no hassles.

Which is pretty much how your typical middle schooler thinks.

Like the adult narrator from *Wonder Years*, I tend to revert back to my teenage psyche to cope with life's most pressing challenges. Why? Because it's where I feel most comfortable.

At age 13, I was on the cusp of manhood, but I knew I was still a boy. It was the last stage in life when there wasn't much required of me — and I loved the freedom. I recall anticipating what was to come with mixed emotions. I sensed I was on the verge of something great, but I was also scared and confused. Most of all, I remember wishing I could just stay right where I was, soaking it all in for a while longer. I knew the step toward manhood would demand more of me, and I wasn't so sure I wanted to go there — or even if I could.

During middle school, I knew things were changing, but the whole manhood thing seemed way beyond me. My body was growing. More and more was being expected of me and I resisted the changes. I liked being a kid. It was fun hanging out with my friends, shooting hoops, playing video games, and living without any real responsibility. I remember looking at my dad's life and thinking it looked hard. It also looked boring. He got up, went to work, and came home. Every day.

In one episode of *The Wonder Years*, young Kevin asks his dad to summarize his life. The father replies, "I get up at 5 a.m., I fight traffic, I bust my hump all day, I fight traffic again, and I come home. And I pay my taxes."

That wasn't what I wanted for my life.

Deep down, most teenage boys feel the same way. It's a very confusing time — physically, emotionally, and hormonally. It's all happening at once. Even the young men who seem so confident are fearful of the transition to manhood. I remember having lots of questions, but I was afraid to ask them. Even though my dad was available, I never thought he'd be open to the conversation — not to mention I had no idea how to start it!

––––––––

In the ABC comedy *The Middle*, an episode called "The Man Hunt" captured the bewilderment that teenage boy's experience. The 13-year-old son Brick (that's his name) actually asks his dad the manhood questions that most teenage boys wish they could. After going to a friend's bar mitzvah, Brick comes home asking about his own rite of passage and questioning why his parents never did anything for him. He wants to know if he missed an important ceremony for his own manhood. He's perplexed how his Jewish friend (who is younger and smaller) is somehow dubbed "a man" while he's still standing on the sidelines watching.

Like most adult men, his tongue-tied dad has no language to convey what it means to be a man. He fumbles around, trying to talk about responsibility and courage. He even takes his son to work with him, but in the end, he has nothing to offer about manhood. Finally, in utter desperation, the dad buys Brick a plaid flannel shirt (like his own) and teaches him the art of flipping burgers on the grill. It was a bittersweet scene. Sadly, all he had in his toolbox were clichés on how to be a man.

This fictional sitcom hits close to home.

Today's dad just doesn't have a good definition of what it means to be a man. So he says nothing. As a result, the current state of father-son relationships is short on substance.

The silence is deafening.

————

As a man, I am still wrestling with my inner teenage boy.

My younger self is alive and well. And I am constantly re-training him on what it takes to be a man. He can be a little resistant at times, but he's still teachable. When he wants to take the easy route, or tempts me to keep life nice and simple, I challenge him to up his game.

Truthfully? I don't want to kill the "Kevin Arnold" who lives inside of me. He reminds me to not take myself too seriously and enjoy the simple things in life. He gives me optimism and a thirst for something greater.

Admittedly, he can be irritating — showing up at the wrong time with the wrong information. And the wrong impulse. When he does, I ask him to step to the side and let a man do what needs to be done. But sometimes, I'm sad to say, I still allow the 13-year-old in me to have too much say-so in areas he shouldn't.

Growing up, I never knew there was such a thing as a masculine code of conduct that could propel a man forward in life. Actually, I didn't have a masculine paradigm to guide my life until I was in my 40s! Because I found out so late, I didn't want my own boys to wonder about their manhood and wander through life in quiet desperation.

I wanted them to know the *essence* of a man and the *actions* of a man — so they could rest comfortably in their own masculinity and enter high school (and life) with confidence.

Although equipping my sons was the main driver for *ManQuest*, I've come to realize that I also wrote the book for the little boy who lives inside of me.

And perhaps inside you, too.

The Secret Lives of Teenage Boys

I was living in "La La Land."

Not the Oscar-winning movie, but the dreamy obliviousness of an average dad.

One day while my son Chase was in middle school, he told me I had "no clue" what was going on in his life. Those words cut me to the core. Not only was he telling me I was out of touch, but that I wasn't even in the game. There's nothing more confounding to a man than feeling powerless. We get frustrated and befuddled when our words and actions don't have any impact. As men, we want to have it all together. We want to be the source of truth, the fountain of wisdom.

This was a huge red flag for me as a father.

Hey, wait a minute, I wrote a book on leading teenage boys into manhood. I have all the answers, right? Wrong!

As dads, we often have no clue what our teenage sons are dealing with below the surface. For me, it was much easier to live in "La La Land" and assume that Chase was immune from all the junk that goes on in teenage boy world. From that point on, I started listening much closer.

In some shape or form, all middle school boys are facing decisions about pornography, bullies, cliques, drinking, drugs, vaping, explicit music, violent video games, sexting, cheating, stupid stunts, and other challenges. It's easy and natural to believe that *your* son is not involved in any of this, and hopefully he's not. But I guarantee he's under massive peer pressure. If he has just *one* guy in his circle of friends that's involved in negative behaviors (he most likely does), he's having to make big choices *right now* ("Do I go along? Do I take a stand?").

It's a good bet he feels stressed out and alone in the process … and you are clueless.

Behind that tough guy exterior or blank expression is a hunger to confide in someone. Too many young men feel like they have nowhere to go to share the details of their life. Most teenagers stop telling their parents what's going on in their lives due to peer pressure. If by chance a boy shares something with a parent who has loose lips and it gets out on the "parent wire," there's usually hell to pay for the poor kid who had the audacity to confide in his folks.

Teenage boys are notoriously vicious at putting each other down and exploiting any weakness in their "friends." Therefore, most middle school boys are in lockdown mode on sharing info with their parents. Here's the good news: *ManQuest* provides a great conduit for sparking conversations to get teen boys talking with you about what's really going on in their lives.

————

Boredom and fear are the two predominant emotional drivers for teenage boys.

That's according to Ted Braude from his book *How Boys Become Men*. And most adults will never know this. Why? Because the Boy Code mandates young men must wrestle with their boredom and fear on their own — in silence.

Teenage boys are a special puzzle because they rarely give parents a glimpse into what they're thinking or feeling. At home, they're usually sulking and lazing around, making sure everybody knows they're just "chilling" — with a phone or remote in one hand and a game controller in the other. This body language says, "I'm unavailable for meaningful dialogue."

If this hasn't happened in your household yet, just wait — it's coming!

Braude says that parents, educators, coaches, and influential adults often miss that teenage boys are tired and bored of the same old scene and are craving something fresh and new. While we can't fathom how they could possibly be bored with such an array of stimulating entertainment choices at their fingertips, they are tired of the "same-old same-old." And that includes just about anything from mom, dad, and teachers. For a lot of young men, the family dynamic is old hat and the school grind isn't taking him to new places.

A middle schooler doesn't want to be treated like a little kid anymore, and feels entitled to the rewards of adulthood — without actually taking on any new responsibility. He's restless and bored, but because he still needs his parents for survival, there's no available escape hatch in the foreseeable future.

This underlying teenage conundrum impacts countless families every day.

————

No offense, but your teenage son probably finds you boring.

It's not your fault, but you aren't very exciting to him anymore.

Braude says your son is a "student of the game" and has been watching you in action for years. In his mind, there's not much left to be learned on the home front. There's a great big world out there for him to discover, and the family dynamic feels old and all played out. He likely feels typecast and trapped in whatever role he's been playing since he joined his family. If you think back, his mood is not too dissimilar from how we felt as kids.

We were bored, too.

Teenage boys have traditionally been bored in the classroom and in the family. That's old news. But now they are getting bored in the one area where they use to be able to exert their playfulness and raw energy — the *sporting field*.

Kids used to play multiple sports and enjoyed something new and different each season. Now, with the pressure to specialize in one sport (to become the best), kids aren't getting the diversity of experience they once had. Throw in personal trainers and year-round travel teams, and kids are getting burned out and bored with one of the last bastions of spontaneous, creative expression for boys.

In addition to the decline of purely recreational sports in our culture, there's an overall shortage of meaningful activities for young men. Teenage boys require appropriate "proving grounds" to test out their new-found physical strength, emotional depth, and creative expression. But sitting in front of a TV screen, laptop, or cell phone will never give them the guidance, direction, and challenge they desperately need.

————

Teenage boys are a strange paradox.

On one hand, they are begging for something new and different to propel them forward. On the other hand, they are scared witless about the mystical journey ahead of them. So it's not uncommon for them to vacillate from fear and withdrawal one moment to cockiness and independence the next. This often leaves parents scratching their heads trying to figure out what's going on.

In *How Boys Become Men*, Ted Braude tells parents to look beyond all the bluster, obnoxiousness, and clamoring for independence.

I agree. The tough guy act is a smokescreen to distract adults from recognizing what's really going on — fear of failure, fear of rejection, and fear of the unknown. Too often, grownups buy into the charade and have no idea how to respond to the mixed signals they're receiving. One thing's for certain — a teen boy will never admit he's afraid. Boys feign indifference and act like they don't care in order to distract adults, friends, and girls from their underlying fears.

Want to know why your teenage boy seems apathetic? Because he is protecting his image and covering up his fear. To him, it's better to act like he doesn't care than to try something and fail at it.

Truth is, boys usually have no idea *why* they do *what* they do. They only know that showing fear is not an option. Early in life, they learn from peers (and misguided adults) that expressing fear is simply not allowed. Fear is an emotion, and emotions are considered a sign of weakness for teenage boys. So they stuff it all down and hide any external clues about what they're feeling.

What exactly are teenage boys afraid of?

Braude says, "Pretty much everything."

1. Among his *friends*, he's working hard to fit in and carve out whatever identity is acceptable to the group he's seeking to impress. His popularity within that group is fragile and can fluctuate from moment to moment without any rhyme or reason.

2. *Girls* trigger an entirely different set of fears in teenage boys. While he may be wildly attracted to the opposite sex, they also unleash something he's deathly afraid of — feelings.

3. Above all, teenage boys are afraid of the *future*. When they look down the road, the outlook is ambiguous at best, threatening at worst. While their body is telling them it's time to grow up, they know that being a kid requires much less effort and seems way more fun. At their core, they wonder if they have what it takes to make the journey to manhood.

In 1904, Scottish author J.M. Barrie wrote a bestseller called *The Boy Who Wouldn't Grow Up*. You know it better as *Peter Pan*.

Peter, of course, is the boy who doesn't want to mature, and lives in Neverland where young men romp and play as "eternal boys." Today, Peter Pan Syndrome is the term for men who are unwilling or unable to grow into maturity. They are adults physically, but they lack the motivation and self-confidence adults need to assume normal responsibilities. By clinging to adolescent fantasies, they reject the realities and difficulties of adult life.

Oddly, the disorder is limited almost exclusively to the *male* population.

This "Peter Pan" phenomenon is becoming almost the norm in our society. It's common for movies, TV shows, and commercials to both support and glorify this sad trend. Delaying manhood and responsibility has become a badge of honor for many young men in our society. Think of all the "classic" movies that glamorize it — *Step Brothers, Failure to Launch, Grown Ups, Old School, Wedding Crashers,* and *Jeff Who Lives at Home.*

There's only one solution: Adults must help our next generation overcome their fear by painting a picture of manhood that's fresh and exciting and attainable.

———

"Every kid is just one caring adult away from being a success story."

That's according to Josh Shipp, a youth motivational speaker and TEDx Talk superstar.

So true. Every young man needs and deserves to have one older man who believes in him, invests time with him, and conveys positive messages.

A father, coach, grandpa, uncle, brother, mentor, or teacher can have a significant and lasting impact on the trajectory of a young man's life. All it takes is some directed and intentional attention. Caution: While teenage boys certainly need affirmation from older men, be careful not to heap on too much praise just to bolster their self-esteem. Teen boys have a great "BS detector," and nothing makes them cringe faster than false flattery. It's important that dads and mentors "keep it real" with their teenage boys.

Boys need to know that life is no longer all cake and ice cream — that more is required of them. During those crucial years, somebody needs to challenge them, call them out, and help them make sense of things when they are sluffing off or making a reckless choice.

Remember, men are made, not born. Teenage boys need to encounter something (or someone) they can't manipulate or control. They don't respect or appreciate anything they get for free, so somebody needs to keep putting "price tags" on things for them and encouraging them forward.

––––––––

Your son doesn't need another buddy. He needs a father.

Many adult men try to re-live their youth through their sons. Hence the trend of "buddy dads" who want to be a *peer* rather than a *guide*. In today's fathering, there seems to be a higher premium on being your son's friend than ever before. I know for a fact the concept of "being my friend" never hit my dad's radar screen when I was growing up. He knew his job was to *raise me up* and *coach me* along toward self-sufficiency.

I hear dads proudly boast that their son is their "best friend." I get that. Friendship is a great long-term goal as your son matures into adulthood. But it shouldn't be the driving force during his adolescent years. Friendship connotes personal intimacy and shared responsibilities between two equals. And quite frankly, there'll be times when a young man needs tough love, firm accountability, and a stern wake-up call that a friend or peer *cannot* deliver.

There are times when a dad needs to push his son out of their comfort zone and into the unknown. This action usually creates tension, and if a dad worries too much about the "friendship" aspect, they might hold back on what needs to be said. That's the challenge — to find the balance between encouraging boys to give greater effort and letting them know you believe in them and care deeply.

On one hand, you can't be a "hard-ass dad" all the time and have a positive relationship with your son.

On the other hand, a "buddy dad" isn't respected at crunch time.

The answer lies somewhere in between. It's a tough tightrope to walk, and I'm constantly trying to strike the balance.

————

What's your favorite adventure movie of all time? *Braveheart? Pirates of the Caribbean? Jurassic Park? Avengers?*

Action flicks like *Black Panther* or *Justice League* naturally resonate with the built-in male desire to cut loose and take chances. Especially to young men!

Teenage boys yearn to be tested and pushed past their limits. But it's getting tougher to find activities these days that take young men out of their comfort zones and into the wild. A trip to the mall or the video arcade or the Cineplex doesn't cut it.

It's one thing to be told you have what it takes. It's another thing altogether to discover that you actually *have* the "right stuff" through some trial (during an adventure) or through some test (during hard work). Today's young men enjoy a false sense of control and comfort because most of life can be accessed with the touch of a cell phone, joystick, or keystroke.

Things like organized sports, robotics club, marching band, and youth groups can teach important life lessons, but at the end of the day, they are *structured activities.* Watching sports, playing video games, and attending concerts are fine father-and-son activities, but they are *passive entertainment.*

Today's teenage boys need to encounter the wild — to go where life is unstructured and unpredictable and anything can happen.

As fathers, we can be so wrapped up in our own work and leisure time that we no longer take our boys outdoors to share the lessons that only nature can teach. Men, opportunities for adventure with our sons are all around us — kayaking, camping, fishing, canoeing, mountain biking, hunting, hiking, whatever.

When my son Chase was 14, we rode ATVs in the Rocky Mountains on a father-son bonding weekend. Miles from civilization, we encountered a particularly treacherous incline. It had snowed that morning, and the slick layer of snow and ice covering the rock in front of us gave me pause. *Do we go for it?* I quickly flashed back to the rental guy telling us "not to push it." *Do we take the risk?* I also remembered the long list of fees and fines if I damaged the vehicle or got it stuck. My son asked what we should do. I responded with bravado: "What's the worst that could happen?" With a whoop, we plowed forward up the mountain.

Probably not the brightest thing I've ever done, but certainly one of the most exhilarating!

Before you get the impression that I'm some chest-pounding macho dude on a rant about pushing the limits, it's important to note that I am pretty much a coward. Growing up, I resisted any and all attempts by my dad to teach me "manly" things. One day, he wanted to teach me to ride a motorcycle — *No thank you*. Another time, he tried to show me how to fire a gun — *Not interested*. Finally, he suggested a white-water rafting trip — *Again, no thanks*. Truthfully, I was afraid.

Looking back, I wish I would've agreed to those one-on-one times with my dad. I missed out. I was resistant. If your son says no, I would encourage you to push through the fear (yours and his) and find something adventurous you can do together.

Craigslist Rent-a-Dad

Dig deep enough into the psyche of any middle school boy and you'll uncover three pressing questions about manhood that he's dying to ask an older man, but probably never will:

1. *How do I become a man?*
2. *How is a man supposed to act?*
3. *Do I have what it takes to get there?*

These questions — always bubbling just below the surface — shape just about everything middle school boys say and do. The sad part is, they rarely get addressed for the majority of teenage males.

Not long ago, a fascinating advertisement popped up on Craigslist. It was placed by a group of guys searching for a "BBQ Dad" to handle the grill at their outdoor party. My teenage son, Chase, thought it was hilarious and shared it with me. While it's obviously a joke, it's actually a great commentary on the real-life yearnings of young men in our society and their desire to be mentored ...

> *To interested individuals — We will be throwing a backyard BBQ on June 17 to celebrate beer and each other. We range in age from 21-26, and while most of us know how to operate a grill, none of us are prepared to fill the role of "BBQ Dad." That being said, we are in need of a generic father figure from 4-8 p.m. Duties include:*

• Grilling hamburgers and hot dogs (whilst drinking beer)
• Referring to all attendees as "Big Guy," "Chief," "Sport," or "Champ" (whilst drinking beer)
• Talking about dad things, like lawnmowers, building your own deck, Jimmy Buffett, etc. Funny anecdotes are highly encouraged (all whilst drinking beer)

We can't pay you in money, but we can give you all the food and cold beer your heart desires. Grill for a few hours, then sit back and crack open a few cold ones with the boys. This is a real ad. Do not hesitate to call if you are interested.

This tongue-in-cheek ad contains some not so subtle Millennial mockery. The writers are poking fun at the lifestyle of Baby Boomer Dads — whose traditions they are trying to avoid at all cost. No doubt they are taking some degree of comfort by employing some humorous irony in their ad. At first glance, they sound like pampered college grads with limited life skills who are looking for somebody to serve them (for free). But if we delve a little deeper and look beyond the sarcastic tone, there's something else going on here.

It's pretty obvious these young men are crying out for an older man to come alongside and show them the way. It's easy to read between the lines and see they feel ill-equipped to handle the responsibilities of manhood. They are seeking guidance from a wise sage. In their own words, they admit that "none of us are prepared" to handle the responsibility of grilling. Which is code for "none of us are ready to make the transition into manhood and we need some help."

The humorous ad has little or nothing to do with needing a "grill-meister." Asking for culinary guidance makes sense if they were throwing on some steaks or something a little more ambitious — but burgers and dogs? No, they are begging for an older man to come to their party and show them how a man is supposed to act because they're feeling lost.

What they're actually saying is, "Living in the real world is pretty dang hard and there's got to be more to this 'man thing' than drinking beers with the boys. We don't know how to express our needs fully, so please look beyond our childish ad and come point us in the right direction."

Did you notice the gig was from 4-8 p.m.? If it was just grilling they were after, it could all be accomplished in 30 to 60 minutes. Why do they want BBQ Dad to hang around for an extra three hours *after* the grilling? Because what they really want is the companionship and mentoring of an older man.

They want him to hang around and "crack open a couple of cold ones" because they need true masculine energy and wisdom. It's easy to see through their smoke screen of requesting a "generic dad" who will spout cheesy nicknames and talk about mundane topics. What they really want is to "grill" an older male about the journey they are facing with uncertainty.

It's no coincidence that their party took place on Father's Day Weekend.

If a boy doesn't get answers to the three fundamental questions about manhood during his middle school years, doubt and confusion will linger in the recesses of his psyche for years to come. If he's never equipped with manhood tools, he'll probably end up sitting around at BBQ parties, drinking beer with his friends, trying to do "man stuff" — all with a nagging suspicion that a key part of his masculinity is missing.

It's up to fathers, grandpas, uncles, coaches, teachers, and mentors to make sure the young men in our lives won't ever need to hire a "stand-in" from Craigslist to help them figure out something they should have been told by us.

————

I remember sitting on a couch in my therapist's office feeling completely lost.

At 28 years old, I was newly married to an amazing woman and I was making more money than I ever imagined. I owned a great house and had an active faith. All the boxes for a happy life were checked off, but I still felt empty and hollow inside and had no idea why.

It's not uncommon for uninitiated men to hit rock bottom at some point and have no clue why they're in crisis. In my case, we had just been in a devastating car accident that required my wife to have surgery. During this emergency, it became obvious that I had no emotional support or strength to offer in her time of need. It didn't take the counselor long to realize that I was "Mr. Cellophane." I had no sense of my masculine core and you could see right through me.

I was a collection of what I thought I *should* be and what everybody else *wanted* me to be.

After serious reflection, I realized that I had married my wife partly because I wanted her to show me how to become a man. While this may seem strange, it's not uncommon for uninitiated men to try and draw strength from their partner to "fill in the gaps." My wife possessed many of the qualities I admired and wanted for myself. She's a self-assured, adventurous, risk-taking, straight-talking, passionate person. Although it may seem kind of crazy, deep down I was hoping some of her strength would rub off on me.

After a year of marriage, it wasn't working. Why? Because no matter how powerful femininity is, it can never bestow masculinity. Not to a teenage boy and not to a full-grown man.

Fortunately, my counselor helped me start searching for my masculine voice. He believed in me and taught me what a man is supposed to say and do in this world. And most importantly, he told me I had what it takes. He told me I could have my life back, and he taught me how to fight for it. He helped instill courage and strength in me for the first time. I stopped looking for my wife to show me the ways of manhood, and I charted a new course for my own life.

As a result, I made some major changes. In fact, I changed just about everything (except for my wife!). But even this was just a "stake in the ground," as it took many more years to find my masculine footing.

Many times, it takes a major life event to shake us out of our comfort zone and hit the reset button. The purpose of *ManQuest* is to give a teen what he needs upfront, so he never has to waste valuable years groping around (like me) and going back to square one (like I had to).

Since that initial tipping point, I've been fortunate to have a number of older and wiser men teach me, challenge me, and spur me on.

So, what *does* authentic manhood look like for me? Truthfully, it can ebb and flow. But on my better days, it looks something like this:

1. I put my ego aside and choose love.

2. I live with a purpose or a cause that is greater than myself and beyond my own comfort and pleasure.

3. I live in the here-and-now and don't get overly focused on the past or the future.

4. I give space to the people I love so they can relax in my presence and be fully themselves.

5. I resist my desire to control outcomes; I allow things to unfold naturally and enjoy being surprised.

6. I step into difficult and uncertain circumstances and use my strength where it's needed.

7. I'm willing to leave my comfort zone and try new experiences and embrace new challenges.

8. I'm vulnerable and allow people to know me at a deeper level, sharing my feelings freely.

9. I speak truth by saying what I need to say, when I need to say it.

I'm convinced that a man feels most like a man when he puts his heart on the line and gives his time, talent, and treasure to somebody or something greater than himself — taking risks and possibly failing and looking stupid.   A man uses his strength and power to bring goodness and healing to a world that's in desperate need.

Man Card Wanted

Where can a guy apply for a Man Card?

And what's it take to become a member? How much are the dues?

Unfortunately, you can't just sign up or join a club to become a man. There's no sanctioning body or rules committee. Becoming a man is an individual experience that is not for sale.

If someone *could* bottle "manhood," it'd be worth billions.

Why? Because if we're honest, most of us live with underlying doubts and uncertainties about what it means to be a "real man." Deep down we're always questioning our manhood to some degree. In 2016, the international survey firm YouGov published a report that asked men to rate themselves on a masculine scale. Approximately 65% of men approaching retirement age and 30% of men ages 18-to-29 identified themselves as "completely masculine."

Is it any wonder we try to fill in the gaps with all sorts of foolish pursuits to make us feel manlier — only to come up empty.

Bungee jumping, skydiving, jet packs. There's a reason the Adventure Sports Industry is a multi-billion-dollar enterprise. From rock climbing to motocross, guys are into "extreme sports" in record numbers. I believe this thirst for adrenaline and danger is a substitute for the initiation rites that young men go through in other cultures — often involving feats of strength, courage, and endurance. The instinct for initiation is alive and well in today's young men, but without the guidance of a reliable mentor, it manifests itself as risky behavior.

To somehow "legitimize their manhood," many teens (and adults) get hooked on crazy, daredevil adventures, often risking life and limb.

In his book, *Man Made: A Stupid Quest for Masculinity*, Joel Stein, a 40-year-old journalist for *Time*, pushes himself into new and uncomfortable places — like Marine Corps boot camp, firefighting, sparring with a mixed martial arts fighter, Wall Street trading, and so on. Stein hoped some of the macho action might rub off on him, so he could someday pass on that "manhood" to his newborn son. As a dad, it's natural to want to convey manly wisdom to our sons, and having a baby is often a trigger to check your testosterone gauge. Predictably, doing hardcore man stuff did not help the writer become more of a man.

But give him some credit! Stein's *Stupid Quest for Masculinity* was an intentional (albeit futile) attempt to find the elusive Holy Grail of manhood. We can chuckle at the notion of such a quest, but most of us guys spend our lives chasing after the same thing — only we don't even *realize* we're doing it.

Contrary to popular beliefs, you don't automatically become a man when you reach a certain age or reach some milestone. You don't become a man when you buy your first car, grow facial hair, have your first sexual experience, get a tattoo, graduate college, get married, buy a house, make your first million, or climb Mt. Everest. And you're not automatically a man just because you possess certain equipment between your legs.

Manhood isn't so much a permanent condition, but a series of ongoing choices we make. The more we choose to live as a man, the more confident we become and the more naturally it flows from us. Manhood is built on daily, hourly, minute-by-minute decisions each guy has to make for himself. That's why it's so essential for every man to have a masculine paradigm to guide him through life.

Becoming a man is an on-going, lifelong process. You never quite fully get to the top of the "manhood mountain" to beat your chest and proclaim "I've reached the peak!" In reality, the journey *is* the destination. I'm in my 50s and I'm still growing in my manhood. I hope you are, too.

———

As Zig Ziglar famously said, "If you aim at nothing, you'll hit it every time."

ManQuest provides a target to aim for — a bullseye that helps us zero in on the essential actions of a man. Lots of people will judge you on their own self-created "manliness scale" that has no stated criteria. If you don't have a clear and compelling definition, chances are you will pursue a lot of crazy ideas trying to prove them right or wrong.

In **Section 2** of the book, I offer a "masculine north star" to help us navigate. I call it "The 5 Guideposts," and it's the heart and soul of *ManQuest*. In short, the Guideposts spell out the essential actions of a man. Ultimately, my ability to rise up and take these actions propels my manhood forward. Same for you.

Someone said you can't steer a canoe that isn't moving.

As men, we don't do well when we're motionless and stuck in neutral.

We are made to move forward and push into difficult situations with uncertain outcomes! We're wired to bring order, goodness, and value to our families, schools, faith communities, and society.

My transition to manhood hit overdrive when I stopped thinking like a little boy who always expected things to be easy and comfortable. Soon after, I started to embrace difficult challenges with a willingness to see them through.

Too often, my main goal in life is my own comfort or entertainment.

When the going gets tough, my natural reaction is to go underground and play it safe. But I never learn anything or grow as a man by withdrawing from a challenge. Today, I feel most like a man when I'm stretched beyond my limits — not for my own selfish ambitions or thrills, but for another person or a cause I believe in.

We all have plenty of opportunities in our daily lives to use our strength, power and ingenuity to bring healing and comfort to the world around us.

A few years ago, we were celebrating my daughter's fourth birthday at a place called Jungle Java — a play and climbing attraction for kids. As Trinity was running around with her friends, she threw her favorite stuffed animal up in the air. Against all odds, "Puppy" somehow fell through a small space between a large paper mache tree and a climbing platform.

Her beloved friend dropped eight feet into the bottom of a fake tree. There was no way to get him out. Trinity was absolutely devastated. Outside of her family, Puppy was the most important thing in her life. Actually, Puppy *was* part of our family. She carried it with her everywhere she went. I wanted to rescue him, but I couldn't see any way to get that little guy back.

I asked the folks at Jungle Java if I could cut a hole in the side of their fake tree and reach in to retrieve him. (I'm sure their legal department had a good laugh with that suggestion.) My daughter was beyond upset. Despite having a fantastic birthday party with her friends, she had lost her "security blanket." She tossed and turned all night and cried most of the next day.

It was heart wrenching to see her so sad.

I tried many harebrained ideas to get Puppy back, but none of them worked. One week later she was still in misery, and the memory of Puppy hadn't faded. I kept racking my brain for a solution. Finally, I had it! I procured a light-snake and a video monitor (used for diagnosing clogged pipes), so I could locate him at the bottom of the tree. Then I dropped the light and a skinny vacuum hose down into the tree until it was right on top of Puppy. (By the way, he was laying on a stack of other stuffed animals and toys sharing the same fate.) I flicked the switch and sucked Puppy up. When I finally got that little guy in my hands I felt like a million bucks.

The reunion party between Trinity and Puppy was euphoric. She squealed, danced around the house, and talked to Puppy in their own special language. I had used my ingenuity and determination in a challenging situation for somebody I love. Not the stuff that wins medals, but I never felt manlier in my life!

The Most Interesting Man in the World

One of the most memorable ad campaigns in history was "The Most Interesting Man in the World" for Dos Equis beer. The commercials featured a fictional spokesperson who tapped into male fantasies of money, sex, power and adventure. Played by American actor Jonathon Goldsmith, the ultimate "man's man" sold a lot of *cervaza* over the years.

The narrator on the commercials shared humorous and outlandish stories about the most interesting man's masculine qualities and exploits, including:

- *"His blood is like cologne ... hurting him only makes him more desirable."*
- *"He's so smart ... he's the only person to ever ace a Rorschach test."*
- *"His charm is so contagious ... vaccines were created for it."*
- *"He's so good with the ladies ... a casual glance is considered a first date."*

The genius of these ads was that although viewers knew they were a farce, they captured our imagination and somehow made us wonder if a six-pack of barley and hops might help us achieve our own "true" male identity.

Why did the audience love him so much? Taking cues from James Bond, "The Most Interesting Man in the World" was suave, debonair, and obviously rich. He was a captain of industry, and an adventurous gambler who got the most of out of life. He uttered pearls of wisdom and demanded only the best. Of course, he was always surrounded by beautiful young women (Goldsmith was 78 when his last ad ran in 2016!) hanging on his every word.

And oh, yeah, he drank Dos Equis.

Give credit to the ad agency for achieving what most beer ads strive to do — accentuate the lies of false masculinity and prey on the insecurities of men. Over the years, we've been inundated with dim-witted guys and scantily clad females telling us how "real men" should live. The only constant seems to be that you need a cold brew next to you at all times.

––––––

Growing up, I always thought the coolest accolade you could get from your peers was to be called a "Man's Man."

Being a Man's Man meant winning the esteem of the men around you without trying too hard. It was a confident attitude you acquired through years of successful refinement. As the saying goes, "Every woman wants to be with him and every man wants to be him."

A Man's Man was cool, confident and bold. His combination of manly skills and no-nonsense personality distinguished him from his more feminized counterparts. In my mind, a Man's Man didn't complain, brag, or sweat the small stuff. They were tough, sensible and logical. They didn't mind roughing it, but behaved like gentlemen with old-fashioned values. Other guys were respectful (and envious) of a Man's Man because they always had the solution for any problem.

Thanks to Hollywood, my image of the consummate Man's Man was a guy who could saunter into any establishment in the land, pony up to the bar, and attract a host of new friends and admirers. He'd buy drinks for guys he doesn't know, and keep them captivated with saucy jokes and tales of his exploits. He'd be well versed on all subjects from sports to politics. He'd be a hard drinker and a tough fighter (when needed). The party started when he arrived and ended when he left (with the most beautiful woman on his arm).

His money never ran out and his charm never faded.

Believe it or not, that bundle of clichés had been my masculine idealization for as long as I can remember. I never felt I had what it took to *be* "that guy," but subconsciously he was the target I was shooting for. Deep down, I always wanted to be a Man's Man. That's probably true for most guys, too. How about you?

––––––

Researchers have coined a term for this rigid set of expectations that define what a "real man" is. They call it the "Man Box" because it confines and restricts men to an acceptable set of societal behaviors and penalizes them for venturing out. According to the Good Men Project (*goodmenproject.com*), "A real man is strong and stoic. He doesn't show emotions other than anger and excitement. He is a breadwinner. He is a heterosexual. He is able-bodied. He plays or watches sports. He is the dominant participant in every exchange. And whether or not we'd actually want to spend time with him, we all know who he is." Society passes on the tenets of the Man Box to the next generation from the very beginning of a boy's life. It's called the "Boy Code."

Dr. William Pollack defines the Boy Code as "a set of societal rules and expectations that come from outdated and highly dysfunctional gender strategies — the idea that boys need to keep their emotions in check; that violence is an acceptable response to emotional upset; that their self-esteem relies on power and they must reject any and all signs of feminine qualities. Boys learn it and then police each other's behavior, keeping one another in check and isolating those who don't fall in line. The Boy Code is a powerful societal force that's hard to alter or escape."

We perpetuate the Boy Code every time we tell a young man to "man up" or "stop crying like a baby" or "you're acting like a girl." As a society we inadvertently use these harmful phrases without weighing the damage or thinking about the consequences they have on a young boy's psyche. Language matters. We need to be very mindful of what kind of messages we are passing on to the next generation of men.

———————

Let's face it, most of us measure manhood in three ways — financial success, sports achievements, and sexual conquests.

We are pounded by these messages nonstop. No wonder there's a male identity crisis in our country. Most men can't thrive within the pop culture definition of manhood, so they fail in their efforts or stop trying altogether. More and more men are realizing they don't have the right stuff to compete in a world that falsely defines masculinity as sports success, attention from women, and wealth accumulation.

So they opt out.

Younger men tend to drop out of the high-achiever rat race and settle for life in their parent's basement. Some older men may try to numb themselves with coping mechanisms like drugs, alcohol, or porn. Others turn to more "socially acceptable" hobbies, like food addictions, consumerism or sports gambling. This explains why depression, suicide, and substance abuse in middle-aged men are at all-time highs. Society is changing all around us and today's male is, for the most part, still languishing in the Man Box.

Guys, there has to be more to life than career advancement, fantasy sports teams, adventure sports, golf addiction, weekends in Vegas, car shows … and porn.

Right?

Many of the things we call hobbies are actually distractions and time killers — placeholders for what we really want but can't put into words. Deep down, we all know these diversions are not the measure of a man, yet most of us struggle to see outside this brand of counterfeit masculinity. Because these lies have been fed to us since birth, we live in a state of confusion.

The lies start young and accumulate as years go on. Adolescent boys are taught that athletic success equals manliness. Teenage boys are told that "getting girls" elevates their status as a man. Adult men are told that job titles and big paychecks determine their value in society.

According to Joe Ehrmann, the primary "proving grounds" for what's perceived as male success are the *ballfield,* the *bedroom,* and the *boardroom.*

No wonder today's predominant male mantra is, "He who dies with the most toys wins."

Sadly, that pathetic statement sums up our goal as men. We live in a "compare and compete" culture where everyone is always trying to "one-up" the next guy. We're taught to play a zero-sum game, an equation where for me to win, you must lose. If you have something of perceived greater value than me, then I want it — and anything goes on how to get it.

One summer, I saw this scenario played out in perfect form. My wife and I were out to dinner. While we were outside waiting for our table, something interesting happened. There was a shiny red Lamborghini in the parking lot. It was jaw-droppingly cool. As we waited for the next 30 minutes, I can't tell you how many men walked up to that Lambo and ogled it. They walked around it, stroked it, and snapped selfies with it.

The comments I heard oozed false masculinity. Some debated which superstar athlete was in the restaurant (Sports — the *ballfield*). One guy piped up, "Find the most beautiful woman in the restaurant and the car's owner is with her" (Sex — the *bedroom*). Some guys boasted to their buddies and said, "I'm going to get me one of those someday" (Wealth — the *boardroom*).

The "most toys" mantra was on full display.

Every day, we spend physical and emotional energy on things that really don't matter and neglect those that should matter most. What would happen if we made a point of intentionally living outside the Man Box and modeling this for our boys? What if we focused on "exploring our essence" instead of falling for societal clichés?

No doubt we would pass along something more real, true, and noble to our sons.

————

Today's male (more than ever before) has the freedom to live *outside* the Man Box's rigid design. And dads, we have the power to help our boys chart a new course. But it needs to come from us first. Is your concept of masculinity something akin to the "most interesting man in the world?" Looking back, I've unintentionally taught my sons some pretty warped and outdated masculine messages over the years. More recently, I've come to realize there's not just one set of male characteristics to aim for. And being male no longer means denying the traditionally feminine attributes we possess.

It used to be that men who were well-rounded and knowledgeable about many subjects were the most admired. These "renaissance men" traveled extensively, conversed in multiple languages, appreciated culture (art, theater, literature, poetry), discussed philosophy and religion, and had an appreciation for music, film, and entertainment. Men used to define themselves by their breadth of life and prided themselves on exploring new areas of learning and competency. Over the years, the concept of the renaissance man has become less appealing as we lead more narrow, focused lives built on technology and rigid stereotypes.

Somewhere along the way, we lost our "depth of being." As men, we tend to be quite good at deflecting — making jokes out of serious issues in order to keep things light and superficial. Today's man uses humor and irony as defense mechanisms to avoid facing any real problems or emotions. It's a strategy of disengagement that keeps men isolated and alone.

If adult men were completely, brutally honest, I believe the vast majority would say they don't have one real friend in the world.

Today's man is more apt to define himself by the things he *doesn't* do rather than what he's all about. We have "knee jerk" responses to certain actions we deem unmanly and resist them instinctively. We've been trained by the culture to put rigid masculine and feminine labels on most things. And we teach this to our boys. In fact, it's become socially acceptable for men to have hideaways called "man caves" where we can retreat back into our narrow masculine world. It's in our "man cave" that we try to reconnect with our masculinity through isolation, cigars, sports, porn, junk food and/or alcohol. Even if we don't have a physical basement hideout to retreat to, most of us have built a "man cave" in our minds.

We know there's a better way to live, but don't know how to get there.

Escaping the Man Box

Gender roles are rapidly evolving in our society. Today's man has more freedom than ever to explore life outside the narrow box he's been living in. There's not just one way to live as a man. Research shows the next generation of men are rejecting a socially prescribed set of behaviors that keeps them confined to traditional patterns. Their views on relationships, work, finances, faith, responsibilities, child-rearing, etc. are vastly different from their fathers and grandfathers. For instance, it's become far more common (and socially acceptable) for men to raise the kids and not be the primary breadwinner. While shifting gender roles will continue to have seismic ripple effects in our society, the main benefit is that men and women are enjoying far more flexibility to choose their own path in life.

Gender roles are socially constructed but also have a biological basis. It's hard to deny there are natural masculine and feminine energies embedded in our cosmos that weren't created entirely by social norms:

• *Feminine energy* is creative, fluid, flowing, vulnerable, feeling, intuitive, nurturing, collaborative, receptive, personal, intimate and relational.

• *Masculine energy* is rational, focused, stable, linear, ordered, protective, problem-solving, controlled, physical, competitive, results-oriented and hard.

Unfortunately, society has separated the two energies for thousands of years and provided little guidance for women to express their masculine energy and men to engage their feminine energy.

Today, the cultural curtain is being lifted and men are learning that getting in touch with their feminine energy doesn't make them any less of a man (and vice versa). We are all a unique and wonderful blending of both energies. Even if a guy has a lot of female energy, the male body is designed to put male energy forward, so there's masculinity just from being in a male body. The same is true for females.

Sadly, a lot of men will fight any attempt to attach anything feminine to their identity. That's a shame because they are missing out on a key part of their personhood. Women are far ahead of the guys in getting in touch with their parallel energy. There's a lot we can learn from the ladies.

———

Did you know that all males have estrogen (the primary female hormone) pulsing through our veins, in addition to testosterone (the primary male hormone)? It seems like we're designed to be in touch with our feelings and emotions, as well as to be rough and ready.

Being male means living a "whole life" — with an all-encompassing range of emotions and experiences. We can break free from the narrow and rigid code we were handed in our youth and the box we've been living in as an adult. I hope this message is a little unsettling, scary, and exciting … all at the same time.

Regardless of age, it's never too late to chart a new course. The first step is to embrace your uniqueness. Take time to reevaluate what you truly enjoy doing, without putting any labels or judgments on them. Ask yourself: *What activities would I pursue if nobody was watching?* Then go for it!

Is it easy? No way!

I'm still struggling to punch myself out of the cardboard container (the Man Box) I've been living in for all these years and get more real with myself. I'm taking baby steps. But for the first time, I'm free to admit that this 6'6" corporate VP enjoys going to a Broadway musical as much as watching football. I like a glass of chardonnay as much as a triple malt scotch. I can wear a pink shirt without feeling self-conscious. I prefer a Frappuccino to a black coffee. And yes, *The Bachelor* is one of my favorite TV shows. I'm a work in progress but I am getting more and more in touch with my emotions, even getting tearful in times of great joy or sadness.

I know some of you are probably judging my masculinity right now. That's okay. But please know that none of these interests or expressions make me less manly. I'm free to enjoy all sides of me. And as a result, more of my true essence is emerging. That's what I want my sons to see and emulate.

I think *that* guy is far more interesting, anyway.

The Times They Are a Changin'

Bob Dylan sang that back in 1964. And the times are *still* changing.

Faster than ever, actually.

There have been countless societal changes since I first wrote *ManQuest* in 2010. When I survey the ongoing shifts in our cultural landscape, it's literally staggering. And many of the changes are making it even more difficult for teenage boys to become men of decency and honor.

The exponential growth of instant communication and unlimited access to information are having a huge impact on our sons. It seems like every teenager now has a mobile device glued to their body and connecting them to the world. Teens are instantaneously and universally aware of happenings in the world (both good and bad), and plugged in 24/7 with their friends to discuss it.

Teen boys are inundated with so much more of, well, *everything* than ever before and they are becoming jaded by the nonstop overexposure. So they clam up. It's much more challenging now for parents to create meaningful, face-to-face connections with their kids.

In the last decade, five big shifts — happening simultaneously — are reshaping our culture (and our parenting):

1. First, a teen's perspective on the world is more apt to be influenced by social media and their misinformed friends than by parents. Our voice is diminishing rapidly. It's increasingly hard for kids to hear the message of traditionally influential adults above all the noise. Parents need to be more intentional than ever with what they want to communicate. (Unfortunately, many adults are too distracted by their own mobile devices, but that's a separate issue.)

2. Girls are thriving and boys are mostly stuck in neutral. Over the last 25 years, girls have been told they can do and be anything. And they're taking it to heart! Young ladies now get 61 percent of the college degrees in America and boys get 39 percent — a complete reversal in just one generation. Single women are now buying homes at 2.5 times the rate of single men. This trend is so pervasive, a recent study showed that 80 percent of aspiring parents prefer a daughter to a son. Girls are taking over the world. Boys are struggling to get it in gear.

3. There's been a lot of talk in the recent years about gender and sex. The two words used to mean pretty much the same thing. But the concepts of male-female, masculine-feminine, and man-woman are fading. The "sex" of an individual is considered binary and based on biological characteristics like chromosome, sex organs, and hormones. Using that criteria, 99.9 percent of humans are male or female. However, "gender" is no longer rooted in science, but based on societal norms and belief systems that an individual most identifies with. Gender today is fluid and totally dependent on the person.

Last time I checked, Facebook had 58 different gender classifications for members to select from. As a result, there's more confusion than ever on pronoun use because the words "he" or "she" no longer apply to everybody. Some parents are now raising their kids as "theybies" — by not disclosing the sex of their child and raising them without gender norms. Society's stance on traditional norms and gender stereotypes is changing rapidly. Fewer and fewer people view masculinity as a reliable (or even appropriate) paradigm.

4. The "Me Too" Movement has boldly brought male misogyny into the light. More and more men who've used their power and influence over women are being held accountable for their sexist behavior. It's not okay for men to use influence and position to manipulate women for sexual favors. The "old boys

network" has been exposed, and those who've gamed the system are going to jail, losing their careers, being sued and publicly disgraced.

5. Kids have less time to "just be kids." Between school and extracurricular activities, teens have way more pressure and far less time to cram it all in. These days, if you don't get tutoring and perfect grades, you might not be accepted to an elite college. If you don't get year-round private sports training, you might not make your high school team. If you get an MIP (minor in possession), it goes on your permanent record — and could keep you from getting a good job someday. Future employers and colleges are now checking social media posts to evaluate the character of their applicants. No matter what kids are involved in these days, the stakes are higher and the societal drive for kids to excel is far more intense.

As a result of this drive for perfection, families have less quality time together, and kids are more stressed out than ever. Teenage anxiety and depression are at all-time highs, and I blame it on adults. Jealousy gets the best of us parents when we hear friends brag: "*Hailey made the elite travel team that's going to nationals … Hunter has the lead role in the play … Spencer takes advance math classes at the university.*"

Sound familiar?

As adults, we push our kids to not only keep up with the Joneses, but to crush them. And all those hours of practice to "be the best" takes its toll on our kids. When teenage boys *do* have time on their hands, it's no wonder they check out violent video games, explicit music, and pornography for relaxation (all with their own set of bad consequences).

———

I tell you — it's *tough* being a teenager in today's world.

There's never been a more difficult and dangerous time to be a young man in our society than right now. In my generation, the majority of kids waited until high school to experiment with drinking, sex, and smoking pot. Now we're seeing *middle schoolers* dabbling in all three!

Did you know that one out of four kids in the U.S. will have sex before they hit high school? And about the same percent will drink alcohol before they get out of middle school?

Think of how different things are today. Did you ever think heroin would become a recreational drug for teens and an epidemic among suburban students? Could you ever have imagined kids texting screen shots of their genitals to each other? Ten years ago there was no such thing as vaping, and now every teenager is having to make a choice whether to follow the crowd or not.

It's sobering to think that it's now considered a "divine right" for kids to have a mobile device and a data plan with unlimited access to the internet — and all its content, filter free. Heck, when I was a kid, I'd pedal five miles on my bike just to see a *Playboy* magazine. Now we give our boys an X-rated world of pornography at their fingertips. And we expect them not to look?

Man, it's *tough* being a teenager in this society.

And boys seem to be in even greater crisis than girls. The teenage suicide rate for boys is four times higher. Boys are five times more likely to die from homicide. Boys are twice as likely to be diagnosed with ADHD. And as we saw earlier, less than 40 percent of today's college grads are male — a complete reversal from 40 years ago.

Obviously, more and more young men are struggling to find their footing and getting sidetracked on the journey to manhood. As we noted, it's now acceptable for males to arrive at maturity and independence much later in life — some in their mid-20s to early 30s.

That's *long, long* after boys are biologically and developmentally ready to become men! The Peter Pan story has become all too real and we wink at it, like it's cute or funny.

Special Section: Message to Moms

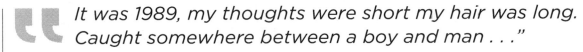

It was 1989, my thoughts were short my hair was long. Caught somewhere between a boy and man . . ."

— From *All Summer Long* by Kid Rock

The "*somewhere between*" is one of the most turbulent times a mother will face.

Moms and sons share a special bond. Throughout childhood, mothers give of themselves time and time again to meet the emotional, physical, social and intellectual needs of their boys. Then one day, when that magic switch of puberty turns on, a boy's focus turns inward, and she becomes almost invisible to him. Since the dawn of time, women in every culture have felt this unexpected pushback from their sons. This shift is incredibly annoying and heartbreaking, both at the same time.

At this crucial transition, moms should back off and give their son some breathing room. Instead, many make the understandable mistake of pushing even closer — trying anything to restore the relationship back to a steady state. Sadly, this "smothering" often backfires and pushes the boy away. While it's natural for moms to want to regain their prominence in a boy's life, it's critical to recognize he's asking that their relationship change.

Speaking of change, in middle school everything is changing for a boy — his body, his voice, his mysterious attraction to the opposite sex. It's all evolving, and so must his relationship with mom. Do you know how uncomfortable it is when hormones start raging in a teenage boy? He's developing into a man (complete with newfound sexual stirrings), yet the primary female relationship in his life is his mother. Can you say *awkward?*

Of course he's going to be asking for some distance!

Ladies, when your son starts to spread his wings, you must realize that your role as a mom is shifting. I know this may seem rather harsh. But if you can accept your new place in his life, you will save yourself a lot of heartache and actually forge something beautiful and rewarding.

Fighting too hard to hang onto the past can cause deep-seated bitterness and long-term resentment in a teenage son. If mom doesn't give her son adequate space during his manhood transition, feelings of anger and disappointment can develop. This tension can hang around the edges of a mother-son relationship well into adulthood.

It's important to underscore that moms are crucial in the healthy development and maturation of young men. However, she is the last person a boy wants to learn about "man stuff" from. Moms have extraordinary insights to share, but a *ManQuest* journey requires active direction from somebody who's personally been down the same road he's getting ready to travel.

While moms can offer invaluable perspectives on manhood, they do so only from the vantage point of an outside observer.

In his book, *Father Fiction*, Donald Miller talks about growing up without a father and the deep masculine void he experienced through adolescence and beyond. Miller recalled how his mom did the best she could to fill the gap, but wasn't equipped to give him what he needed to become a man. Growing up without a masculine model created confusion, skepticism, rebelliousness, and self-doubt. Fortunately, in his 20s, a male mentor stepped into his life and showed him the ways of manhood, firsthand. Today, Miller is a bestselling author and founder of The Mentoring Project, a nonprofit that partners with local churches to mentor fatherless young men.

————

Moms, here's my best advice for you: As puberty approaches, the wisest thing is to "read the tea leaves" and accept a modified role in your son's life. Openly acknowledge to him that you're glad he's becoming a man, and that it's okay for your relationship to grow in new ways. By doing so, you're honoring his maturity and showing your son you believe in him.

Remember, you are still hugely important — but with a different job description. If your son doesn't currently have a trustworthy adult male in his life, invite somebody to take an expanded mentoring role. During adolescence, it's imperative that your son has a relationship with an older man who thinks (and shows) that he is worth the time and effort.

If your son is shutting you out, or being mean and nasty, don't despair. It could be his way of asking for something different in your relationship.

In *How Boys Become Men*, Ted Braude says that as long as a boy feels like his mom still "needs him," he won't move onto manhood — he will hang out in the shadowy zone between childhood and adulthood. He is torn. He loves mom like crazy but knows he needs something new … and doesn't know how to express it.

So, in a strange and confusing paradox, he tells her how much he loves her by hurting her.

If your son is making you crazy with his antics, remember that he is afraid of his own developing power, and reacts by bringing fear and destruction to others. In the Boy Code, fear is unacceptable. So he resorts to what he knows works — damage and pain. He will say and do things, whatever it takes, to get mom to back off.

As I said, when a son pulls away from mom, she will often respond with what has always worked best — more love and more support. I've watched my own wife struggle with our boys. While she understands the bigger picture and their need to move on, she still uses pet names to draw them closer, or makes special meals to show her love, or buys them gifts, etc.

And then she gets frustrated because they don't treat her better!

"Look at all the wonderful things I do for you," she says. And it's true. But boys don't respect *anything* they get for free. So they only appreciate her thoughtful gestures momentarily. As soon as they realize that part of mom's motivation is to create emotional connection, they flee right back to their old patterns. It's a vicious cycle that goes nowhere good until a mother can make a major paradigm shift in her expectations and evolving role.

So what's a mother to do?

Recognize that your son loves you too much to bluntly tell you he needs something different — so *you* must be the one who initiates the difficult changes. Braude says that a mom's best strategy is to become "Queen of the Realm." In other words, mom needs to come first. Mom needs to demonstrate her strength and position in the relationship. Let him know she is not just there as his servant or domestic help. Anything he can do for himself should be done by him.

How does the "Queen" protect her throne? By maintaining strong boundaries in how her son speaks to her, and clear expectations of his responsibilities around the house. Enact tangible consequences if he doesn't deliver and follow through. (Don't ask your hubby to be the heavy. Find your strength within!)

This will not be easy; he will surely fight you on the changes. And the battle lines are blurry. While part of him wants to be more independent, he's also very accustomed to the comfort you provide.

Once again, it has nothing to do with you! It's just a matter of what he needs most.

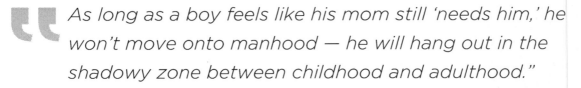

As long as a boy feels like his mom still 'needs him,' he won't move onto manhood — he will hang out in the shadowy zone between childhood and adulthood."

— Ted Braude, *How Boys Become Men*

———

Modifying your existing role will go against every maternal instinct.

Letting your son grow up requires courage and introspection. After all, you've only ever known him as your little boy. That's why it's tough to change-up your relationship and implement some "hardcore mothering." You've invested 12-plus years of love and support and nurturing into this guy, and to shift gears so he can move on to manhood will be one of the toughest things a mother must do.

But to stay where you are — having him fight you tooth and nail — is no picnic either. Ultimately, he needs to hear that you feel he is strong and capable and respected. He needs to be encouraged to get out there in the big world and try new things, because you're his biggest fan. And when your boy gets wounded in this thing called life — as he surely will — he needs to know mom is not going to swoop down and rescue him or fix his problem.

When your teenage son circles back to you with his failures and troubles, you need to give him two very strong "mom" messages:

- You'll always be there to listen.
- You believe he has what it takes to handle whatever challenge comes his way.

Moms have a sixth sense when it comes to the needs of their children. When it comes to *ManQuest*, most moms usually "get it" right away. In fact, many women have read the book first and then spurred their husbands to read it and take their son on the *ManQuest* journey.

More than ever, women are eager for ways to better understand the masculine psyche — because it's so foreign to them. Moms are looking for direction on how to deal with a teenage son who no longer wants to be their little boy. If that's you, ask your husband to step up. If you're a single parent, give this book to a trustworthy male and ask him to mentor your son.

In summary, give your boy room to grow, but hold him accountable for his actions. It's tough to strike this balance, but it will allow something fresh and promising to blossom in your relationship.

Let him know you'll always be there to listen, and that you believe he has what it takes to handle any challenge."

— Mike McCormick

NOTES

Top 10 Reasons to Do *ManQuest*

Too busy. Too tired. Too nervous. Coming up with excuses is easy.

Don't let that skeptical voice in your head keep you from the most important experience you'll ever share with your son. Don't let your fear of the unknown handcuff you. Your son will benefit immensely from this experience and you are the perfect person to guide him. It doesn't matter if you've made mistakes in the past, or feel ill-equipped to lead him.

Trust me, you have everything it takes to complete the journey.

Here are 10 reasons to take your young man on a *ManQuest* journey:

1. One day he'll tell you it was the most meaningful thing you ever did together.

ManQuest sets the stage for a lifetime of conversations. And guess what? One day, when you least expect it, he'll come back to you and say that this adventure was the most important thing you ever did together. Remember, this is a long-term process with an amazing ROI (Return on Investment). You are literally planting seeds that will continue to germinate for generations — and will leave a lasting legacy.

2. Your son will never have to wonder if he "has what it takes."

Don't assume your son knows you believe in him and think he has what it takes to become an awesome man. *ManQuest* is a tangible way to tell him without a shadow of a doubt that you believe in him and that you are there for him. These words need to be spoken and then backed up with an experience that underscores your belief in him. And he will carry your words with him for a lifetime.

3. MQ reduces the likelihood he will repeat the mistakes you made.

Let's face it. We've all done things we're not proud of in life. ManQuest asks adult men to engage their sons in dialogue and open up about their mistakes. Like it or not, the "sins of the father" tend to get passed down to their sons. If we can openly share our failures and teach the lessons we've learned, it reduces the likelihood they'll repeat our errors. If we say nothing and just "hope they do things differently," there's a good bet they'll follow us down our darker paths. Teenagers know us better than we think, and we can unwittingly pass along our worst tendencies to our boys. It's better to be up front and honest about your past.

4. MQ helps him wrestle with the deeper questions of life.

ManQuest is a conversation starter. If an adult male opens his heart and mind to the experience, he will be surprised where the dialogue will lead and the topics you'll cover together. It's important that your son gets to know you, what you believe, and the roads you've traveled. Sharing life stories is a powerful tool that can open up new channels of communication on life and living. Remember, you are always in charge of the *ManQuest* material and what you want to talk about or not. Read the material and decide how you want to present it.

5. MQ helps create a pack of friends that will influence each other as they move into high school together.

ManQuest can be done one-on-one with excellent results. But it works best when done with a group of friends from school, youth group, Boy Scouts, sports teams, etc. Friends play a big role in our kids' lives. Peer pressure is huge. If one friend is heading down a dead-end road, he usually drags some of his buddies with him. If boys share the same masculine code of conduct and deepen their relationships through group activity, they'll have a positive influence on one another. Young men who experience *ManQuest* together move into high school with a stronger peer group and an extra shot of confidence.

6. MQ is an easy way to spark important conversations that won't occur otherwise.

"How was your day, son?" You know the response — a shrug, then crickets. It's hard to engage in meaningful conversations with teenage boys. Outside of school, activities, or friends there's not a lot of subjects to engage them in. Taking your son on a *ManQuest* journey provides a context for deeper conversations that simply wouldn't happen on their own. You'll be amazed at how much you'll learn about each other.

7. Time is of the essence — your voice will diminish once he enters high school.

Timing is everything. There's a wonderful window of influence open between the ages of 12 and 14 that we absolutely need to seize. If you hesitate, you may miss it — and never get it back. Middle school boys soak up new information like sponges *and* still naturally want to spend time with their dads. When they hit high school, our window of influence shrinks considerably. Or closes altogether. Seize the moment while it's still there.

8. Culture and peers have already "programmed" your son with a false brand of masculinity. He needs to hear a strong counter message from an adult he trusts.

By now, I hope we all agree we're fighting an uphill battle against the false cultural messages of masculinity. Young men need to learn about manhood from a man who can help sift through all the lies out there and give them something they can bank on. They appreciate it when somebody takes time to help them chart a new course.

9. Although they may act like they know it all, teenage boys inwardly hunger for influential men to show them the way.

There's a hunger inside every man to hear words of affirmation and love from a father figure. Every man, no matter what age, wants to be mentored by an older man, especially their father. Heck, I'm in my 50s, and whenever my dad reaches out and asks me to do something, I will drop everything to be with him. That never changes. Feed that hunger.

10. MQ initiates open communication at the beginning of the tumultuous teenage years — *before* the inevitable teenage crisis.

Don't lead from behind. *ManQuest* is all about being proactive and opening the lines of communication early in the game. We all want to believe our kids will stay on the straight and narrow, but there are no guarantees. There are so many pitfalls out there for young people in our society. More temptations than we can imagine. Establishing a base of communication and talking through issues up front is like basic training before heading into combat.

Final Words: You've Got This!

You don't need to be a Super Dad or have a Ph.D. in fathering to take a young man on a *ManQuest* journey. You just need the courage to step up and step into his life at a whole new level. And even though he may not admit it out loud, this is something your teenage son definitely wants … and absolutely needs.

Remember, a young man won't do this on his own, and he won't ask you for it. It requires your active leadership and willingness to make this happen.

One of the biggest mistakes a dad can make with *ManQuest* is to ask his son if he wants to go on the journey. This is a gift you are giving to him, so there's no need to ask. It's up to you to take the first step and make it real.

While he inwardly thirsts to be shown the way to manhood, he's probably scared to death and will feign indifference or just plain say no. Young men simply don't know what they want or what's best for them. He needs to hear from you that it's something *valuable* that you really want to give to him.

When an adult man tells a teenage boy that he wants to give him the roadmap to manhood, something profound stirs inside that young man. He won't know what that stirring is about. It may even scare him. So be ready that he might fight you on it. He may make fun of it or act like he doesn't care. Sarcastic humor and apathy are a boy's tools for covering up fear. If this happens, stay the course and trust the process. Don't let his teenage qualms keep you from giving this gift.

Note: If you're reading *ManQuest* and don't have a teenage boy in your life, I encourage you to reach out to a young man who doesn't have an at-home father. There are plenty of Big Brother or mentoring programs out there to engage with. If your son is past that prime middle school age for ManQuest, don't give up. It's way tougher to get his attention, but still totally worth your time and energy.

––––––––

There are 3.5 billion males alive on the earth. What would this world be like if there were less men walking around with a gaping hole in their soul from the most undiagnosed (and deadly) disease in our society — *father hunger?*

What if men were released from the never-ending cycle of validating our "self-worth" through power brokering, sexual prowess, or wealth accumulation?

What if we taught manhood to every teenage boy with the same urgency that we teach math, science, and English?

It would fundamentally change our society forever … one man at a time!

The ultimate measure of a man is not where he stands in moments of comfort and convenience, but where he stands at times of challenge and controversy."

— Dr. Martin Luther King, Jr.

NOTES

Section 2:
The Roadmap

 When I was a child, I talked like a child, I thought like a child, I reasoned like a child. When I became a man, I put the ways of childhood behind me."

— The Apostle Paul writing to the Corinthians

Getting Started

Every man, no matter what age, needs a clear and compelling definition of manhood to guide him through life. I've designed "The 5 Guideposts" to be a reliable roadmap to help you lead your son's journey.

They are the heart of the *ManQuest* experience.

Each Guidepost chapter is interactive, so any father or mentor can easily start a conversation about the actions of a man. Simply get together with the young man once a week (grab a breakfast or a burger) for five weeks. Each time you meet, you'll take an hour and read through one Guidepost chapter and discuss the questions. For extra benefit, get a group together — your son's friends and their fathers — and discuss each of the 5 Guideposts together over five weeks. A group could also be a sports team, youth group, Boy Scout troop, whatever.

The questions are designed to spark a dialogue about manhood, so don't just breeze through them. Take your time and share your perspectives and life experiences openly.

To kick it all off, we ask each adult man to share his life story with the young man he's guiding. Men, telling your story puts a stake in the ground and sets the tone for the entire experience. Vulnerability encourages vulnerability. Your story communicates that you want him to know you in a much deeper way. That's a euphoric feeling for any teenage boy.

Near the end of each Guidepost, I tell a personal story from my own life to illustrate the point. Hopefully, my stories will spark a memory or two from your own life to share.

Storytelling is an ancient practice, a visceral form of communication that takes conversation to a whole new level. Long before television, radio, and internet, men would sit around campfires or dinner tables and tell stories. In the process, they passed along valuable information to the next generation.

Storytelling links us to our past and provides inspiration for our future.

Over the years, my own kids have begged me to share my childhood memories. It's something all children are curious about. Your openness will set the stage for deeper conversations and a richer experience. Go ahead, give the gift of yourself! You'll ignite a powerful connection as you invite your son into your story — to understand your joy, pain, love, and heartaches. He will forever see you with a new set of eyes. He'll understand where he came from and where he can go. He'll feel less alone and less afraid. Your story will strengthen him.

At the end of each Guidepost, you'll find a "Movie to Watch Together." You could say movies are the language of our culture. Viewing them together is a great bonding experience. I've selected classic films that capture the essence of each Guidepost to help hammer home the point and further the conversation. Discussion questions will help you along. Have fun and make a night of it.

I'm so excited for you to start this journey of a lifetime. The book will guide you along, so just relax. Open your heart and mind and enjoy the experience!

> *Between childhood, boyhood, adolescence and manhood there should be sharp lines drawn with tests, deaths, feats, rites, stories, and songs."*
>
> — Jim Morrison, The Doors

The 5 Guideposts

This crazy world sends us all spinning in confusion at times. It's inevitable that every man will get lost on his manhood journey at some point. In the midst of life's storms, the Guideposts are a reliable "north star" to help us find our bearings. If you ever wonder what a man is supposed to do or say in any given situation, the Guideposts will serve you well.

1. Lead Courageously

A man takes responsibility and action. He doesn't sit around and wait for somebody else to do what needs to be done.

2. Pretend About Nothing

A man lives in truth and requires truth from others. He says what he's going to do and does what he says.

3. Protect Your Heart

A man fills his mind, body, and spirit with things that are true, noble, pure, beautiful, righteous, admirable, and excellent.

4. Engage in Deep and Meaningful Relationships

A man opens his heart, shares his feelings, and allows others to know him deeply.

5. Stay Awake!

A man is alert and open to what's happening all around him; always searching for the deeper meaning of life.

1. I borrowed the phrase "Lead Courageously" from Robert Lewis, *Raising a Modern-Day Knight*. Tyndale House, 1997.
2. I borrowed the phrase "Pretend About Nothing" from Larry Crabb, *The Pressure's Off*. WaterBrook, 2012.
(I couldn't improve on those two phrases! All other Guidepost content and development is original.)

The Story of Dad

Every man has a story. It may be a comedy, a tragedy, or a heroic epic, but we all have one. There are things we're proud of, and chapters we wish we could erase. Either way, they make us who we are. Never be ashamed of your story, it will inspire others. It's been said that owning your story is the bravest thing you will ever do. And remember, you're a work in progress. The story isn't over; you can still write new chapters.

Boys crave to know their fathers, and they want to learn from our experiences, good or bad. I remember hanging onto every little tidbit my dad would toss out for my brothers and me to gobble up — details about his childhood, military years, sports games, and glory days. Sharing your life story with your son is a crucial step in the process. Don't sugarcoat it, fudge it, or gloss over it.

Caution: When men share their story, there's a natural tendency to accent the good and skip over the pain. Please resist this temptation. Your boy is becoming a man and needs to know all about you, warts and all. In many ways, your mistakes and embarrassments are the most important parts to share. Due to genetics, role modeling, or a combination of both, there's a greater likelihood that our kids will repeat our mistakes. Keeping them in the dark about our struggles doesn't help boys grow into men. Ultimately, sharing the edgy stuff lets a boy know you think he's mature enough to be trusted with it.

Letting him in on who you are — what you're thinking and feeling — will draw you closer together. Show him that it's manly to open your heart and mind to other men.

I would argue that your story (and how you've made sense of it) is the biggest influence on the kind of man your son will become one day. Adolescent boys seem to learn best when their fathers share stories of their most difficult struggles and how they overcame them. There's a good bet he's already picked up bits and pieces of it over the years, but he needs to hear your full story. Sit down and tell him the highs and lows. Tell him the pains, failures, and struggles you've experienced. Tell him the joys, successes, and highpoints as well. Tell him your regrets — and most of all, what you learned from the choices you've made.

Later in the book, we'll talk about why men wear masks to fool the world. This is the time to remove yours. Share what you've learned through trial and error, and what you might do differently if you could do it all over again. Many dads won't take the mask off with their son because they don't want to get knocked off a pedestal, or they're afraid their son would think less of them (or reject them) if they knew the real story.

Even if you're ashamed of parts of your past and just want to forget it, your story is essential to your young man's growth. Trust me, it will help him put together the puzzle pieces of his own life.

Sharing your story with your son does three things:

1. It brings him into the "circle of trust." It lets him know you trust him with the confidential insider info of what makes you tick. That's a euphoric feeling for any young man.

2. It primes the pump for further conversations. When he gets into a jam someday, there's a greater likelihood he'll seek you out for advice (or at least remember how you handled your challenges).

3. It lets him know adversity is part of life, and that he shouldn't be surprised or scared by it. Curveballs happen. Disappointments come our way. We all fail at some point. After hearing your story, he will be better equipped to confidently walk into whatever challenges may arise — and not despair.

Research shows that *resiliency* is the biggest predictor of future success. How do you teach your son to "bounce back" after a difficulty? By sharing your story with all its setbacks, struggles — and comebacks!

Helpful Tips for Telling Your Life Story

Find a time and place where you won't be interrupted or feel rushed. Build it around doing something fun and memorable. Go to a favorite place or do a special activity beforehand.

Tell your story chronologically to provide some context. Focus time on your childhood and describe the highlights and disappointments from your youth. What was your father like? Your school? Relationships?

Choose four or five pivotal moments from your life that shaped who you are today.

Take some time to think through what you want to say ahead of time, but don't write it all out (use the outline on the next page). Remember, it's most important to be natural and not scripted. Include the sad, messy, embarrassing details.

Take about 40-45 minutes, and leave plenty of time for follow-up.

Dads ask me, "Are some things too sensitive to share with teen boys?" It's your call. But I advise you to err on the side of telling *more*, instead of less. If you withhold something important now and he finds out later, how will it affect your relationship? Your trust level?

Welcome your son's questions. Let him know he can ask you anything. But don't feel like you have to have all the answers. It's okay to say, "I don't know." It's fine to say, "There are things I'm still trying to figure out." Knowing that their "manly" dad is still in the process of making sense of the pain in his own life will help an adolescent deal with the difficulties he is sure to face (losing a best friend, getting cut from a team, being dumped by a girlfriend, flunking a class, etc.).

Enjoy the process of telling your story to your son. It will inspire him, protect him, and bind you together.

LIFE STORY OUTLINE

My childhood _____

_____

My dad _____

_____

My teenage years _____

_____

Highlights _____

_____

Disappointments _____

_____

Regrets _____

_____

Significant relationships _____

_____

Guidepost 1:
Lead Courageously

> *A man takes responsibility and action.*
> *He doesn't sit around and wait for somebody*
> *else to do what needs to be done.*

Who, Me? A Leader?

Leadership isn't for only a select few who have the "right" genetic make-up or the "right" life circumstances. We all have leadership potential just waiting to be unleashed. And today, we need strong leaders more than ever! At its core, leadership is all about influence … and we all have the ability to influence others with our words, deeds, and actions. Much of leadership is really about having the courage to step up and push into the challenges of life. Leaders don't shrink away when the going gets tough — they rise to the occasion!

Many people mistakenly believe that leaders have to be loud, obnoxious, and opinionated — the "smartest" guy in the room. In reality, the best leaders are "servant leaders" — quiet, humble, and generous people who want to see others succeed. There are all types of leaders, and you are one of them! Never sell yourself short on your ability to lead.

What ways can you be a leader at home, school, or activities?

_____

_____

_____

_____

Show Up, Stand Up, Speak Up

We have too many passive men in our society, guys who sit on the sidelines of life playing it safe. I know, because my *own* natural tendency is to "check out" when the going gets tough. In difficult or uncertain situations, my first reaction is to grab a bag of chips, hit the couch, and just veg out in front of the ballgame. It's easier to hide than to risk the potential for failure, rejection, and ridicule.

There are times when a man needs to overcome his fear, ignore his doubts, and enter boldly into tough situations. When there's an issue that stirs our heart, or when somebody is being exploited or marginalized in our presence, we must act. A man moves into uncomfortable places and uses his strength and power to bring order, justice, and goodness.

In these cases, a man must confront the inner desire to hide or sneak away to safety. Joe Ehrmann says a man must do three things:

1. He makes his presence known by simply **showing up** wherever he is needed.

2. He takes the difficult step of **standing up** and being seen by all. It's so easy to hunker down in our chairs when we need to get up on our feet.

3. He opens his mouth to advocate for what is right and true by boldly **speaking up**.

Got that? *Show up, stand up, speak up!*

Granted, a man runs the risk of saying something embarrassing, or controversial, or confrontational — but silence is not an option when something needs to be said.

Sometimes men don't speak up because we don't really know what we think! Be prepared. Be a man of thought and conviction. Take time to think through your beliefs on key issues like faith, politics, and social justice. Don't be afraid to state your ideas.

I'm not saying it's easy. It's hard to lead courageously, especially when there's a strong likelihood of pain or failure. It's much easier to run in the other direction. But ultimately, a man knows in the depth of his soul that there are things he must do and he does them.

Was there a time in your life when you didn't show up, stand up, or speak up about something you should have? Did *you* regret it? (How about *you*, Dad?)

_____

_____

_____

Outta da Bleachers and into da Game!

The hardest part about being a leader is taking that first step. Most men never do. Instead, they prefer to sit in the stands and watch life go by instead of getting in the game. Do you know *why* men sit on the sidelines their whole life? Because they are scared — scared to fail, scared to be ridiculed, scared to lose. Life is lived on the playing field, not in the safety of the bleachers.

President Teddy Roosevelt knew this truth. He grew up a pampered rich boy who never lacked anything in life. Bored with luxury, he soon found that nothing is satisfying when it comes too easily. Roosevelt set aside his life of privilege, and actively pursued adventure as a heroic soldier, fearless explorer, big game hunter, prolific author, and famous statesman. He loved courageous people, but he scorned the wimps who sat back and threw stones. He wrote:

> *"It is not the critic who counts; not the man who points out how the strong man stumbles or where the doer of deeds could have done better. The credit belongs to the man who is actually in the arena, whose face is marred by dust and sweat and blood, who strives valiantly, who errs and comes up short again and again . . . who spends himself for a worthy cause . . . who, at best, knows the triumph of high achievement, and at worst, fails while daring greatly . . . His place shall never be with those cold and timid souls who knew neither victory nor defeat."*

One heroic man who lost his life for what he believed was Dr. Martin Luther King, Jr. His life was cut short in 1968, but his prophetic words still ring true for every man:

> *"You may be 38 years old, as I happen to be. And one day, some great opportunity stands before you and calls you to stand up for some great principle, some great issue, some great cause. And you refuse to do it because you are afraid . . . You refuse to do it because you want to live longer . . . You're afraid that you will lose your job, or you are afraid that you will be criticized or that you will lose your popularity, or you're afraid that somebody will stab you, or shoot you, or bomb your house; so you refuse to take your stand. Well, you may go on and live until you are 90, but you're just as dead*

at 38 as you will be at 90. And the cessation of breathing in your life is but the belated announcement of an earlier death of the spirit."

Is there something you need to do but are afraid to try? What keeps you from going for it?

_____

_____

_____

Be a "Yes" Man!

With today's technology, you can enjoy life's comforts without ever leaving your house. We have online shopping and an unbelievable world of entertainment at our fingertips 24-hours-a-day. This is one reason it's so tempting to cocoon indoors and say "no" to new opportunities.

But that cautious lifestyle will stunt our growth! As human beings, we learn by exposing ourselves to new experiences. We grow by saying "yes" to new things and trying them on. If they don't fit, no problem — we can take them off and move on to something else.

The great wisdom teachers say you cannot truly see or understand anything if you begin with a "No." Instead, be a "Yes" man! Be willing to say, "Sure, I'll try it" to new experiences. Warning: Saying "yes" to new experiences may put you into some difficult and precarious situations (and that's the point).

Take risks that will move you beyond your comfort zone and challenge you — like taking a mission trip, being a camp counselor, working toward Eagle Scout, trying out for a sports team, running for class president, starting a lawn service, making a friend with somebody new, etc.

The opportunities to be a "yes" man are endless.

Go ahead, stretch yourself beyond what's comfortable and see what happens. Sure, you could fail. And yes, you could hate it. It may even feel like a waste of time. But better an "oops" than a "what if." On the other hand, it could be the best thing you ever did! A wise man said, "In life, if you don't risk anything, you risk everything."

Condition yourself to say "yes" to new opportunities. Step up to the plate and take a couple of swings. It may not work out. But there may be something new and cool for you to discover. Don't miss it!

When have you said "no" to something you should have said "yes" to? What did you do instead? Do you regret it?

_____

_____

_____

Do Something that Scares You

Courage is not the absence of fear. It's moving forward even when you're scared to death. Courage is mustering the will to take action when there are no guarantees of safety or success — stepping up when you have no idea of the outcome.

The "cold and timid souls" (as Teddy R. called them) do the easy stuff with no risk and no reward. But that's not you. Courage is moving forward despite the urge to quit or turn back. It's giving up your own personal security or comfort because there is somebody or something that needs you.

Is it safe? Make no mistake, a man *will* be wounded. There *will* be casualties among the brave. The only questions are: How will you recover from the wounds, and how will you grow from your pain?

In his book, *Wild at Heart,* John Eldredge says, "A man is never more a man than when he embraces an adventure beyond his control, or when he walks into a battle he isn't sure of winning."

Men have been endowed with strength and power to rise up and bring order and goodness to the world. Sometimes, the first and best conflict resolution strategy is compromise. But sometimes as a man you'll just have to stand up against injustice and fight for what is right. Compromise is seldom an option when you look evil square in the eye.

I used to think that some guys were born with more courage than others, and that somehow I came up on the short end of the stick. I've since come to realize that courage is something you can *develop*. By willfully stepping into challenging and unknown situations, our level of courage will grow. Joseph Campbell once said, "The cave you fear to enter holds the treasure you seek".

Courageous people are just like me and you — but have learned to risk it all and not be afraid to put their heart on the line.

What cause, concern, or issue in your life causes your heart to stir and your blood to boil? If you don't have a cause, how come? If you do, what are you going to do about it?

_____

_____

_____

Be a Servant Leader

If you want to become a respected leader, you must first become a servant. Unfortunately, too many men use their power to force the respect of others. This may work for a little while, but respect is ultimately earned by respecting and serving others first. If you prefer using fear and intimidation to influence others, you will never become a true leader. A man is meant to bless *other* people, not just glorify himself. Great leaders tend to "give it away," not "store it up" for themselves.

Leadership is helping others become more than they think they can be, and reaching heights they never dreamed of. Good leaders give the glory to their teammates, and are genuinely happy when others succeed. Unfortunately, many well-known leaders are motivated by feeding their own ego or by the fear of losing what they've attained.

Can you think of a way you can serve someone today or tomorrow?

_____

_____

Get Moving

Don't just sit there, do something! Men were made to move and unleash their creative energy into the world. Most guys are stuck in emotional quicksand or too afraid to fail. That never feels good. It's time to get on with it.

Quick — what are you passionate about? What stirs your heart? Jot it down and commit to doing something about it. Today. Following your *passion* will lead you to your *purpose* in life. But doing nothing will get you nowhere. Throw caution to the wind and go for it!

My Personal Story #1: No Guts, No Glory

I acted like a coward.

A few years back, my two sons (six and nine at the time) were outside throwing a football around on our quiet cul-de-sac. It was a warm September day. I was working in the house when I heard the loud roar of a motorcycle going by. I figured it was probably just our neighbor taking one of his new toys out for a spin, so I kept on with my work.

As the motorcycle faded in the distance, my boys ran into the house out of breath. Agitated, they blurted out, "The guy at the end of the street almost ran us over with his motorcycle!" My eldest son (never one to exaggerate) said the guy rode dangerously close to them and shouted, "Get out of the way, kids!"

I had an instant and immediate swirl of thoughts and emotions. My first reaction was indignation. *How dare he endanger the lives of my boys! Who does this guy think he is?* My boys could see the concern on my face. And I could see they were waiting for me to do something big, but then fear set in.

I didn't really know the older guy who lived on our street. Sure, we'd exchange obligatory nods and neighborly waves as he drove by our house. We'd exchange small talk during Halloween trick-or-treating, but we never had a relationship. I doubted he even knew my name.

Turned out the "guy at the end of the street" was a big shot. A well-known power broker in the community. A turnaround artist who bought and sold underperforming companies. I'd read about him over the years in local business journals. He was rich and successful, enjoying all the accoutrements of his triumphs. The guy exuded "Type A" confidence and a "bigger-than-life" persona that quite frankly was intimidating.

From what I could surmise about my neighbor, the potential for frightening young kids was not beyond the realm of possibility. In fact, intimidation was probably what he did best and it made him a boatload of cash over the years.

I knew what I needed to do — march my boys to the end of the street, knock on his door, and straighten out the situation. I tried to strengthen my resolve by reminding myself that "I'm the CEO of a successful company, and I'm kind of a big deal, too." Unfortunately, self-guided pep talks rarely work. Fear gripped me even harder. My mind raced. *What would I say? How could I say it without being accusatory? How would he react?*

At this point the boys could smell my fear. They had seen the initial indignation and resolve drain out of my face. I could see they were waiting for their dad to defend their safety and honor. It's what every kid expects and deserves from his dad. My own dad stuck up for me a number of times while I was growing up and it always made me feel like a million bucks. But all I could do was focus on myself and wallow in fear. I went over the details of the incident with them again and did my darnedest to convince them the rider probably wasn't as close as they had imagined, and that he had probably just said, "Hi, kids!"

In other words, I did nothing. By abdicating responsibility and remaining silent, I taught my boys a pretty miserable lesson. My gutless example taught them not to trust their own instincts, to avoid conflicts at all costs, and to create delusional stories in their head to justify pathetic actions.

It was the low point of my manhood.

I immediately knew I had totally wimped out, but still couldn't muster enough courage to take action. The regret from this small but profound incident still haunts me. In retrospect, I'm glad it happened because it smacked me right in the face. It forced me to confront a deep-seated suspicion, something I could never admit out loud — *I didn't believe I had the stuff to be a real man.*

When you get hit upside the head with a deep and ugly truth about yourself, you can do one of two things — confront it head on or bury it deeper. After years of being my own gravedigger, I finally admitted that I'm a "conflict avoider." And at the heart of every conflict avoider is fear. Over the years, I've been wrestling with fear and I'm happy to say I'm making progress.

Movie to Watch Together: *Captain Phillips*

In *Captain Phillips*, a large freighter is taken hostage off the coast of Somalia by a handful of gun-toting pirates. The captain and crew demonstrate leadership and courage as they fend off the armed robbers to protect their cargo and crew.

Discussion Questions:

1. How did Captain Phillips (Tom Hanks) demonstrate the principle of "show up, stand up, speak up" during the hijacking of his ship?

2. Captain Phillips says he's just a regular guy doing his job. How does his humility and willingness to serve help him lead during the crisis?

3. Captain Phillips and Muse give us two pictures of leadership. How are their leadership styles different? Are there any similarities?

4. How does Captain Phillips demonstrate courage when the pirates are trying to board his ship?

5. Captain Phillips puts the needs of his men over his own — even offering himself up to save his crew. What leadership principle does that demonstrate?

6. What are some examples of Captain Phillips showing courage, even when it's obvious that he was fearful?

7. Captain Phillips had to work hard to keep the disgruntled crew together during the crisis. He told the crew that "leaders make hard, unpopular decisions." What were some examples of tough decisions he had to make?

8. How did various crew members demonstrate courage during the crisis?

(Nominated for five Academy Awards. *Captain Phillips*, 2013, Columbia Pictures. PG-13)

The problem isn't me talking. It's you not listening."

— Captain Phillips (Played by Tom Hanks)

NOTES

_____

_____

_____

_____

_____

_____

_____

_____

_____

_____

_____

Manhood is the defeat of childhood narcissism."

— David Gilmore

Guidepost 2:
Pretend About Nothing

A man lives in truth and requires truth from others. A man says what he's going to do and does what he says.

Brand Integrity

Branding is a business term that describes how you make your product stand out in a competitive marketplace. A brand is a name, slogan, design, symbol, or feature that distinguishes one product from another (Think Nike swoosh versus Adidas stripes). But it's not just for companies — it's used by *people*. In today's world, just about everybody is trying to gain attention and make themselves stand out above the crowd. They've crafted a brand strategy for themselves in one way or another because we all care (to some degree) how others see us.

Trouble is, the brand we put out there is mostly just play acting and doesn't reflect our true inner self very well. Let's face it, this crazy world is becoming more fake and more phony all the time. Lots of people are now just "famous for being famous" — without any real talent or accomplishments necessary.

My advice? Don't worry too much about your personal brand and how you look to the outside world. Granted, it's hard not to because we're bombarded with 24/7 messages telling us that "image is everything." Next time you pick out your clothes, change your hairstyle, buy a car, whatever, ask yourself: "Am I doing this to get somebody else to think a certain way about me? Or am I doing it because it's a true reflection of who I am?"

What words describe the image you like to show the world? Is this real?

_____

_____

_____

Be Authentic

Authenticity starts with an honest assessment of what makes you, you. Identify your strengths, weaknesses, beliefs and passions. We all have them. What makes you most special? Embrace your own uniqueness, no matter how quirky or "out there" you may be.

Finding peace within yourself means you'll be less apt to follow the crowd just to "fit in." Easier said than done. To be honest, we all enjoy being noticed, recognized and liked. However, re-shaping your personality to fit social situations is a formula for losing your sense of self. The opposite of belonging is not isolation, rather its "fitting in." But doing stuff just to be part of a crowd will never give you what you truly want. Avoid it at all costs! Invest in relationships with people who *accept you for who you are*, and respect and affirm your special qualities.

There's no such thing as a happy chameleon. If you're always changing your colors to fit into your surroundings, you will find yourself lost and confused and rudderless at some point.

What's the unique and special thing about you that you must hold onto and protect at all costs? How about *you*, Dad?

_____

_____

_____

No Posers

Posers are people who purposely say the "right things" in order to deceive and manipulate other people to get what they want.

We all know people who blow smoke at us because they want something. They spend their time pretending so they can get others to act in a certain way that benefits them. As you know, some folks become very good at this. And they seem to reap benefits. Being a poser can get you a good grade, a new friend, a spot on the sports team, or a promotion at work — but is it worth it? Not if you have to suck up to someone to get them!

Although many will say, "That's just how the world works," don't believe it. It's called manipulation and deceit, and it's just plain wrong. As Wesley, the hero of the movie *The Princess Bride,* expresses so eloquently, "We are men of action, lies do not become us." Basically, he's saying "You don't need to lie to me; I can handle the truth." Or in other words, "C'mon, man, you're better than that." As men, we should just speak plainly and honestly with one another.

Have you ever acted like a poser — telling somebody something to get your way? How well did it work? How does it feel after you've deceived somebody by pretending?

_____

_____

_____

Say it Straight

It's easy to tell some "little white lies" and convince ourselves they really don't hurt anybody. After all, everybody does it, right? Wrong. We must remain committed to tell it like it is at all costs. Practice being a "straight talker" and stop the BS. Let your "yes" be "yes," and your "no" be "no." That simply means there's no wiggle room in speaking truthfully. There's no "maybe" when it comes to keeping your word. People respect men who don't sugarcoat it or twist the truth to get what they want.

Becoming an authentic "yes/no" person takes work:

1. First, it requires making a personal decision to pretend about nothing. No matter how hard it gets, we have to speak truth in all circumstances. We must speak the truth even when it would be far more convenient to lie about something seemingly small or insignificant.

2. Next, we have to be ready to deal with any fallout that may come. I guarantee that not everyone will always like what we have to say when we're speaking our truth. Being a "yes/no" person _will_ bring conflicts we'd rather avoid. I know it's often easier to take the path of least resistance. But that path leads to deceitfulness and confusion.

3. Finally, we must avoid third-party gossip. Don't talk smack about other people in their absence. Often, our first instinct will be to say nothing to a person directly, then complain about them or a situation behind their back. That's not straight talk.

It takes a lot of physical and emotional energy to always speak the truth. But it gets easier with practice. And there are rewards. People known as truth-tellers are more respected and have deeper friendships than pretenders. It can get messy and ugly, but it's the only way to achieve authenticity in relationships.

Important Note: Being a truth teller doesn't mean going around spouting off about everything and everybody. Straight talk has to be handled with grace, mercy, and love for others — even in conflict.

When's the last time you told somebody exactly how you felt about something? How did it go?

_____

_____

_____

Is there somebody you need to have a some straight talk with right now?

_____

_____

_____

Man in the Iron Mask

Have you ever felt completely certain about something, only to find out you were dead wrong? It's so easy to convince ourselves of things that aren't truthful or realistic. Shakespeare said, "To thine own self be true." But we often lie to ourselves. In fact, the easiest person to fool is usually the person staring back at us in the mirror!

How can this be? As humans, we tend to make up stories in our mind to help us thrive and survive. In some strange way, it makes us feel better. We create a fantasy in our minds to protect us from a callous and unpredictable world — and soon we start believing our own lies. It sounds crazy, but it's a coping mechanism we all use.

But we don't just deceive _ourselves_ — we create illusions to hide things from _others_, too. We think we're pretty smart, that we can actually fool others with our deceptions. But often, the mask we create to hide the dark and ugly things we don't want others to see is surprisingly transparent. People see right through us! No matter how committed we are to hiding, the truth always seems to rise to the surface.

Can you imagine living every day with a mask on your face? Would it be so suffocating and annoying that you'd rip it off? Or would you just get used to it? Here's a simple but important truth: _The more we_ *pretend, the more comfortable the mask feels, and the harder it becomes to pull it off.* There's only one way to keep the mask off — by honestly facing the longings, disappointments, and selfishness in our souls ... or in other words, pretend about nothing!

Do you have someone in your life you can share the "real you" with? Someone who will listen and help you identify ways that you might be deceiving yourself (parent, friend, mentor, brother)? How do they help you?

_____

_____

_____

Are you aware of any ways you pretend or hide the real you behind a mask?

_____

_____

_____

Strive to be a man of conviction and integrity. Make sure your outside matches your inside. Make your word your bond. Real men live authentic lives. They know who they are, what they are, and where their passion lies.

You will be tempted to "play the game" to make your way to the top, but beware of gaining the world and losing your soul on the journey. Once you start down this path, it's a slippery slope. Whenever you feel like you can't be real (in any area of life), something is wrong. Don't just follow the crowd; blaze your own trail!

My Personal Story: #2 Badge of (Dis)honor

Back in elementary school, I joined the Cub Scouts.

It's a great organization for raising up young men of character. I loved our weekly "den" meetings at my friend's house. We'd have great snacks and all work together on building projects or fun activities. Best of all, we got to wear this really cool blue uniform. After a while, I noticed that all my fellow Scouts were getting merit badges sewn onto their shirts. I wanted some badges on my empty uniform.

I found out that in order to get merit badges, you had to work at home with your parents to show proficiency in a variety of Cub Scout skills. There were badges for mastering things like knot-tying, simple carpentry, first aid, camping crafts, and other areas. I sat down with my mom and we looked through the merit badge activity book to identify the various skills I needed to demonstrate.

However, instead of having me actually *perform* the activities, my mom simply said, "Oh, you can do that" — and signed off that the task was completed. Her heart was in the right place, but I never actually learned the required skills.

I soon had an impressive collection of merit badges across my uniform. Problem was, I didn't know how to do any of the activities! I loved getting the badges. And I enjoyed the accolades I received from the other parents, friends, and Scout leaders. But on the inside, I felt like a complete fraud. I remember the stress of being at a big Scout gathering and worrying that any moment an adult leader was going to come up and ask me to build a fire or tie a knot and I would have no clue.

That's a lot of anxiety for a young man to carry. What happened? Let's just say I never made Eagle Scout. In fact, I quit Cub Scouts the following year because I hated the feeling that comes with being a pretender.

It never feels good when you're living a lie — no matter what your age!

Movie to Watch Together: *Dead Poets Society*

In *Dead Poets Society*, an English teacher (played by Robin Williams) works at Welton Academy, an elite, all-boys boarding school. He instructs his students how to reach beyond conformity and find their own passions and beliefs.

Discussion Questions:

1. What did Knox Overstreet risk by moving in on Chet Danbury's girlfriend?

2. What did "not pretending" get Knox Overstreet from Chet Danbury?

3. How did it feel for Todd Anderson to not pretend he was happy about his desk set?

4. How did Charlie Dalton prove the difference between a stupid stunt and pretending about nothing?

5. Why did Neil choose to "act" and "play the part of the dutiful son?" Why didn't he take Mr. Keating's advice to confront his dad?

6. Neil asked Mr. Keating if "there was an easier way." Mr. Keating said, "No." Sometimes when you stop pretending, people don't like it and try to put you back where they want you. Why did Neil take such a drastic measure?

7. What interested you about Mr. Keating's illustration on conformity (the one that involved marching)? His lesson pointed out "the difficulty in maintaining one's beliefs in the face of others." What pressure do you face to conform?

8. In the end, Cameron sold out Mr. Keating to the administration to save himself. Some would call him a rat or a narc. Are there times when you should pretend about something to protect someone else?

9. In the last scene, the boys risk their academic careers to support Mr. Keating by standing on their desks. They didn't need to do it, but couldn't pretend any longer. How do you think they felt? How do you think the boys who remained seated felt? What would you have done in the same situation?

(The "carpe diem" classic. *Dead Poets Society*, 1989, Touchstone Pictures. PG)

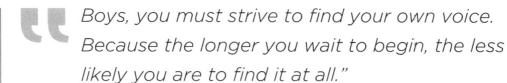

Boys, you must strive to find your own voice. Because the longer you wait to begin, the less likely you are to find it at all."

— Mr. Keating (Played by Robin Williams)

NOTES

_____

_____

_____

_____

_____

_____

_____

_____

_____

_____

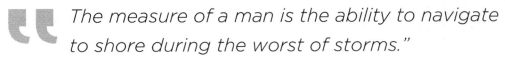
The measure of a man is the ability to navigate to shore during the worst of storms."

— From the movie, *Measure of a Man*

Guidepost 3:
Protect Your Heart

> *A man fills his mind, body, and spirit with things that are true, noble, right, pure, beautiful, ritghteous, admirable, and excellent."*

Cardio Workout

King Solomon has been credited as one of the wisest man who ever lived. About 3,000 years ago, he wrote a collection of wise sayings in the Bible, called Proverbs. In it, he warned us "above all else, guard your heart, for it is the wellspring of life." King Solomon wasn't trying to push some new aerobic exercise or heart-healthy diet to avoid coronary disease. He was saying that the heart is the *core of your being* — your essence. It's where all your hopes, dreams, and passions reside. It's that part of you that connects with God and other people. It's the source of everything else in your life.

Notice Solomon didn't say, "if you get around to it," or "it would be nice if." No, he said to make guarding your heart a *top priority* in life. Why? Because what's stored up in your heart overflows into your thoughts, words, and actions. One of the wisest (and richest and most powerful) men who ever lived thought this was pretty important stuff. And his words ring even truer today in a world where everything is available at our fingertips.

The Good Life

What is the ultimate purpose of life?

Many would say it's to have some laughs, squeeze the most out of every day, and make sure people remember us when we're gone. We live in an entertainment culture that maximizes the fun factor. Having fun is fine, but it should not be our number-one goal. In reality, life is pretty tough, and "most men lead lives of quiet desperation" as Henry David Thoreau said. To avoid the pain of loneliness and desperation, we fill our lives with all sorts of things to make us temporarily happy — toys, alcohol, drugs, TV, pornography, sports, gaming, sex, business success, risky behavior, whatever. We idolize people who seem to "have it all," like sports stars, actors, and musicians. But the "good life" is about more than fame and fortune.

In your opinion, what are the best things in life? How about *you*, Dad?

_____

_____

_____

The things people routinely call the "good life" are really just a bunch of distractions I call the "fake life." The fake life is everything (experiences, possessions, cheap thrills) meant to give you a momentary burst of pleasure — a quick escape so you feel alive and powerful, if only for a short time. The fake life is a mirage that creates the illusion of happiness, but often keeps us from the things that matter most.

How much time do you give to the fake life? In what ways?

_____

_____

_____

Taking Out the Trash

There's an expression computer programmers use — *garbage in, garbage out.*

It means that if we put bad data into an operating system, we're guaranteed to get bad outcomes. Likewise, if we pour sand into a gas tank, a car can't run. What goes into an engine — or a human being — makes a difference!

There's an interesting documentary on Netflix called "Super Size Me" that makes this point. The movie's director, Morgan Spurlock, ate only McDonald's food for 30 days straight. On the third day, he was listless and had no energy. By week two, he had heart palpitations and went to the emergency room. By week three, he was barely recognizable and was puking up Big Macs and Quarter Pounders. He finally had to stop before his liver and kidneys failed. If we put garbage into our body, the output will be garbage. The same is true for our hearts.

Each of us has a 3-pound super-computer sitting on our shoulders. It's called the brain, and it stores reams of data and information forever. While sometimes our memory may fail in recovering some of the stored data, it's all still in there.

Whatever we put into our brain remains there permanently and can impact the way we live.

There are definitely some things I've willingly put into my brain over the years that I now wish I could "delete." Against my will, these images and experiences come back up from time to time to haunt me.

Have you ever gorged or binged on something that made you sick? Was it worth it?

_____

_____

_____

_____

Whatever we put in our brain eventually impacts our hearts. These two physical (and metaphorical) organs have a strong symbiotic relationship — whatever we put into our mind affects the heart and can distort who we really are. Whatever we allow our five senses to experience will be input and stored in our "super- computer" forever. Ultimately, whatever we put into our brains filters down into our hearts.

So what do you put into _your_ heart? That is a decision you must make every day, hour by hour. If you input pornography, explicit music, mind-numbing drugs or violent video games into your brain (garbage in), they will have a direct impact on your heart (garbage out). Don't believe it? Try feeding your brain a diet of destructive input for a while and it _will_ start leaking out — in harsh words, negative actions, and foolish desires.

Lots of men (and kids) tell me, "That stuff doesn't impact me, I can handle it." They are wrong. No matter what age you are, you cannot pack your brain with junk and then shut it down voluntarily to freeze out the things you don't want to think about. Sooner or later, it will affect your thought life and your behavior. To think otherwise is delusional.

You will have "friends" who'll try to get you to do stuff you know you shouldn't. First of all, real friends don't want you to stumble. They just want to feel better about the bad choices they are making, so they are dragging you into their mess. As a teenager or adult, we must make willful decisions to say no to things (and people) that drag our hearts down.

Are there any choices you can make differently right now to protect your heart?

_____

_____

_____

The Slippery Slope

Even the best athletes trip and stumble. The question is not *if* we will fall, but how hard and how fast. And even more importantly, how will we regain our footing again?

It's so easy to be seduced by the fake life. There are nonstop messages out there saying that a fast life of sex, drugs, and materialism will bring happiness. It will be very tempting to buy into that at some point. But you must resist. You must flee. It takes a daily refocus of your heart and mind to stay off the slippery slope. Bad behaviors usually start small and then snowball into an avalanche of terrible consequences.

Have you ever done a little something you know you shouldn't, only to find it spiral out of control and get bigger than you ever imagined?

_____

_____

_____

Job #1 One

Oftentimes, men allow themselves to be defined by their careers. To many people, what you *do* is way more important than who you *are*. As a result, men in our society often pursue a career that gives them the most amount of power and money. Unfortunately, the daily grind drains them of their energy and their life force. It's easy to become a work zombie and give the best of yourself to your job while pursuing the almighty dollar. There's nothing wrong with wanting to thrive in your work, but be careful not to gain the world and give up your heart in the process.

At some point, you'll probably be asked to become something you're not for the sake of money and power. Be ready. An important part of protecting your heart is refusing to trade your goodness and essence for prosperity. You don't have to give in. Fight to stay true to yourself!

As you go through your career, look for a job that's consistent with who you are and that doesn't compromise your integrity. Finding meaningful work and a good paycheck is tough. It could mean choosing a career that earns less money (but then again, maybe not). At the end of the day, work is meant to be challenging, engaging, purposeful and life-giving. If you're going to do something for 30-40 years, why not make it something that enriches your life? And don't let anybody fool you, if you don't like how things are going with work you can always shake it up and change directions. It's your life and you always get to choose your path.

Recently, I went to a high school graduation party and the grad already had his entire career mapped out and his retirement date in mind! On one hand, I thought it was pretty cool that he was thinking ahead. But it was also pretty sad he was planning to hate his career and escape as fast as he could. Kicking back and enjoying life in retirement is a fine goal someday. In the meantime, strive to find a career that helps you to grow both *professionally* and *personally*.

What's your dream job? Why? How about *you*, Dad?

_____

_____

_____

The Road Less Traveled

I know it's tough being a teenager and seeing other kids experimenting with things that seem exciting and fun and "adult-like." There's a natural tendency for teenagers to rush to grow up — but try not to be in such a hurry. Life is long and you will have plenty of time to try "adult things." Enjoy being young for as long as you can! You'll be all grown up before you know it, so relax and enjoy.

It won't be easy to say "no" to stuff when you feel like you're the only kid out there who is choosing wisely. Resist trying to be part of the cool crowd when it means engaging in behaviors that can create problems. Find friends who share the same commitment to making good decisions. They're usually nicer, kinder people anyway because they aren't out to impress others. Do yourself a big favor and wait until you're an adult to try adult stuff. Trust me, it will all still be there in a few years and you'll be far more ready to handle it when you're a little older. Life is long, and making a commitment to protect your heart now will pay a lifetime of dividends.

My Personal Story #3: Barenaked Ladies

When I was kid we didn't have iPhones, and the world wasn't available to us at the touch of a finger. Technology was in its infancy, so we spent a lot of time outdoors looking for excitement and adventure. But *some* things never change …

For most teenage boys, there's nothing more exciting to the eye than the female body. I remember the first time somebody showed me pornography. I was in my elementary school bathroom when some random kid pulled a photo out and said, "Hey, take a look at this." My jaw must have dropped to the floor.

I wanted to see more! After that, I would ride my bike for miles just for a glimpse of naked women in magazines. I knew it was probably something I shouldn't be doing, but I couldn't stop. I even had my own collection of pornography I carefully hid at my home. My friends and I would look at them together and actually rate the women on their physical features.

Hey, it's not unnatural or wrong for males to admire the female anatomy. It's been enshrined for thousands of years in art and sculpture. The human body is beautiful. And sexuality is one of God's greatest gifts for mankind to enjoy. So, was it wrong for me to spend hours of my time gawking and fantasizing about women in magazines?

Yes. Pornography is a destructive force in our society, especially for young men who have no context for sexual understanding. Human sexuality is meant to be enjoyed in the context of an intimate relationship. With pornography, there's no relationship required. You have instant access to beautiful women with no time invested and no hassles. If you're watching a lot of porn, you'll start thinking that's how women are supposed to act. But that's not the real world. It skews your perspective and makes it harder to have authentic relationships with girls.

Remember — what we put into our brain is stored there forever.

That nude photo a kid showed me in elementary school is *still* emblazoned in my mind — and will not go away. Sadly, the countless number of adult magazines I looked at growing up has skewed my view of women and relationships. I wish I could remove the images from my mind, but I can't. Once you've seen it, you can't un-see it. You carry it with you forever.

I've been married 25-plus years, and as a husband I can tell you that the greatest gift a young man can give his future wife is to keep his heart and mind free from pornography. No matter what you've done up to now, you can save yourself a lot of future heartache by saying no to porn … right now!

Movie to Watch Together: *Forrest Gump*

The classic film *Forrest Gump* portrays a simple man who lives an incredible life. As he goes through the decades, Forrest (played by Tom Hanks) stays true to himself and his values during times of chaos. He enjoys a life of rich adventure, meaning, and purpose.

Discussion Questions:

1. When Jenny was a little girl she prayed, "Make me a bird so I can fly far, far away from here" to escape her abusive childhood. How did this pattern play out in her adult life? In what ways did Jenny pursue the "fake life" to ease her pain?

2. Forrest wasn't the smartest guy, but he constantly made good decisions to stay off the slippery slope. While he loved Jenny, he never got swept up in her world. How did he stand above it when others around him were sliding down the hill?

3. What important coping strategy did Forrest learn when he was a little boy that helped him stay away from danger for most of his life? Did he always flee? How can leaving bad situations quickly be a helpful strategy in protecting your heart?

4. Forrest maintains an emotional distance from the world in order to protect himself from the chaos swirling around him, but he wasn't complacent. How did he show incredible love and courage for those he loved?

5. Forrest's momma said, "Life is like a box of chocolates, you never know what you're gonna get." Forrest protected his heart, but he certainly didn't miss out on living an adventurous life. What extraordinary experiences did he enjoy?

6. Lieutenant Dan was angry at Forrest and God because he wasn't able to "fulfill his destiny." What kind of "garbage" did he put into his life to ease the pain? How did he make his peace with Forrest and God?

7. When Jenny left him for the last time, how did Forrest deal with the pain and grief? Why did this prove to be such an effective strategy for "protecting his heart?" What strategies do most people use to deal with pain?

8. Forrest Gump traveled light in this world. He didn't hold on too tightly to anything, especially money. His momma told him, "There's only so much fortune any man needs, the rest is just showing off." In what ways was Forrest generous? Why is it so hard to share our wealth?

9. At the end of the movie, Forrest tells Jenny, "I may not be the smartest man, but I know what love is." Forrest Gump shows us that every person, regardless of intelligence, talent, charisma, or physical appearance, can love greatly and live an extraordinary life. How can you apply this to your life?

10. We are drawn to Forrest mostly because of his general goodness and the love he gave to others. He kept his heart free from the destructive forces around him so he could share it openly with those he loved. Is it possible to live a life like this?

(Oscars for Best Picture and Best Actor. *Forrest Gump*. 1994, Paramount. PG-13)

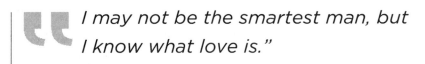

I may not be the smartest man, but I know what love is."

— Forrest Gump (Played by Tom Hanks)

Guidepost 4:
Engage in Deep and Meaningful Relationships

A man opens his heart, shares his feelings, and allows others to know him deeply.

Relationship Muscles

Life at its core is mostly about relationships — who do *we* love and who loves *us*? Someday, when you're on your deathbed, it won't really matter how much power, prestige, or possessions you've accumulated. The measure of a life well-lived is the legacy of relationships that you leave behind and the people you've touched.

Unfortunately, men aren't very good at having close relationships. Most guys will do just about anything to avoid any kind of vulnerability (letting our guard down) or intimacy (letting people get close). Overall, we're pretty lame at putting ourselves out there and creating real and lasting connections with others.

It's not that we *can't* develop deep and meaningful relationships. We just haven't been taught that it's important to exercise our "relationship muscles." As a result, they're not very toned. Why is this? At an early age, us guys are taught to live in our heads and turn off any and all emotions. We are taught that tears are a sign of weakness, and feelings can't be trusted. So we bury our emotions before they ever make it to the surface.

Being perceived as strong and powerful is important to a guy; the worst thing for a male to hear is that he's soft or weak. Adults often use hurtful, damaging words to train boys how to disconnect their heads from their hearts. We learn early on that feelings are bad — that they can't be trusted. That's a complete lie. It's actually very manly to have feelings, express emotion . . . and even to cry.

Feelings are neither "good" or "bad." They just *are*. And they're designed to teach us about ourselves and to guide us.

What are some names people call guys who express their emotions freely? Is it unmanly to have feelings and cry?

_____

_____

_____

A True Friend

The key building block of relationships is trust. Without trust, you won't enjoy a healthy relationship. The people who enjoy the closest and most personal relationships are those who are trustworthy and naturally trusting of others.

Unfortunately, most male relationships in our society are superficial and transactional in nature. If you can advance my career, improve my golf game, or get me tickets to a ballgame, then maybe we can be friends. Sound familiar?

Guys rarely scratch below the surface to find out what makes somebody else tick. No wonder most American men say they don't even have _one_ "real friend" in the world. Sure, most guys have plenty of "good-time friends." You know, fellas to watch sports, play video games, and hang out with. They're good for laughs, but kind of shallow. Finding a real, true friend is a rare experience for men. And there's a sadness that most men carry over not having other guys to share life with.

Men are relationally lazy. We rely too much on women to make the emotional connections in our lives, which is our responsibility, too.

Guys normally don't put much effort into relationships, and then wonder why they don't have any real friends. For some reason, when a man tries to maintain a close relationship with another guy, people often poke fun at him, calling him a "sissy" or "gay." This kind of hyper-masculinity usually starts at a young age, and is quite damaging. As a result, being a "lone wolf" or a "solitary man" is a badge of honor between males in our society.

Men need other men to share the male experience with and to affirm our own masculinity. There's nothing quite like having another man believe in you, confide in you, and give you positive affirmation — as well as be brutally honest with you and tell you when your way off base or heading in the wrong direction.

Do you have a true friend in your life? If not, who are some trustworthy guys you want to go to a deeper level with?

_____

_____

_____

Have you noticed? True, trustworthy friends usually aren't the coolest guy in the room or the best-looking dude or the biggest jock. They're the guy who is there for you when you need him, no questions asked. And vice versa. A true friend is the guy you can talk to about anything and he will listen. And keep it private. He has your back. He knows your weaknesses, calls you on your junk, and pushes you to be better.

How can you be a better friend — especially to your "inner circle"?

_____

_____

_____

Girls! Girls! Girls!

Most males are afraid of girls.

We don't act like we're scared, but girls possess something that frightens us to death — _feelings_. Men typically want to keep things on a superficial level and not deal in the world of emotion — but that's precisely where women thrive. We have a lot to learn from the ladies. Sure, women have a different set of hormones that gives them a bit of an advantage in this department, but that's no excuse. If we want to enjoy the best part of life (happy relationships), we need to work at becoming open-hearted. Being a guy is no excuse!

If you want to be in a relationship with a girl (or even get married someday), learning to share your feelings is crucial. Women connect on an emotional level, so stretching yourself in that area right now is really important. Don't buy into the myth that men don't feel and men don't cry. Women _love_ men who can relate on an emotional level. Actually, if you're going to be happily married someday, it's one of the most attractive and important qualities a man can possess.

Unfortunately, most guys are attracted to girls solely on their physical appearance and don't invest in understanding their hearts. Hey, don't get me wrong, the female body is an extraordinarily attractive work of art, and it's perfectly natural to be excited by its beauty. It's okay to be drawn to a young lady's appearance or physical dimensions, but don't miss out on accessing her heart and her true essence.

For too many guys, the concept of a "real man" is somebody who "gets with" lots of women for their own ego or temporary pleasure. Too often, men treat women as objects to be used and thrown away. While it may seem obvious, it's worth stating that girls are not objects. They are people with real emotions and families who love them. Real men never use derogatory words or talk about women in a way that takes away from their personhood.

As Joe Ehrmann says, "getting with girls" doesn't make you a man in any valid sense of the word. Rather, it simply makes you a "user" of other people — and that's about as low as you can get on the food chain. It's manly to respect women and treat them as equals. A man of honor never feels powerful when another person is powerless, particularly women.

Do you think about girls much? What does respect for girls look like? Do you respect them? Are there ways you can show girls more respect?

_____

_____

_____

_____

The Game of Love

Can we talk about a certain four-letter word?

There's a lot of confusion about the four-letter word that starts with an "L." In today's world, _love_ is mostly mistaken for a three-letter word that starts with "S." It's hard to nail down something as amazing and transcendent as love with a simple Webster's definition, so I won't try. What I _do_ know is that love happens when two people decide to open their hearts to each other in a deep and meaningful way.

Today's culture defines love as taking whatever you can get from somebody else to meet your own needs. Just about every song, movie, or advertisement is telling you that love is all about getting what you want from your partner because you deserve it. That's not love. In reality, love is really about *giving*, not taking, about putting the other person's needs above your own. None of us does this perfectly, but those truly in love earnestly see the best in one another and want the best for each other.

Most of us get our ideas about love by watching movies. In his book, *Love, Sex, and Lasting Relationships*, Chip Ingram describes the "Hollywood model" for love. According to this strategy, we must search and search until we find exactly the "right person." Once we find the girl who meets all of our physical requirements (a hottie), we slip into dreamland and float away on cloud-9 for a happy-ever-after. Ingram says it's a dangerous myth. In reality, we pin all of our unfulfilled hopes and dreams on that person. And when they don't meet our needs and expectations (nobody can) we discard them and go looking for someone new. No wonder half the marriages in our country end in divorce!

Here's a better formula for happy and successful relationships: Instead of trying to "find" the right person, we need to "become" the right person.

Work on becoming a better you by stretching yourself in new areas, like coaching a sports team, going on a mission trip, joining a youth group, doing an Outward Bound experience, or serving at a soup kitchen. Instead of wasting your time trying to "find somebody," invest in new experiences that will help you grow and expand your emotional capacity. Love will naturally flow out at the right time with the right person.

I know you're not thinking about marriage at this point in life. But tuck this away for the future — don't get married until you're ready to place another person above yourself. That's how you know you're ready! Marriage is a lot more giving than taking. When you boil it down, marriage is all about sacrificing for the other person. Someone said, "Marriage is not a 50/50 proposition — that's what *divorce* is." Marriage is giving 100 percent to your spouse (and vice-versa). And there's nothing better than when it works the way it was intended. Wait until you find someone you naturally want to serve … and who wants to do the same for you.

To what degree has Hollywood shaped your view of love and romance — a lot, a little, or none at all?

_____

_____

_____

Let's Talk About Sex

Sex is about the coolest gift God has given to humans. It's the most intimate thing that two people can do together. Sex unifies people physically, emotionally, and spiritually. It is a sacred act that should not be entered into with just anyone. As a result, it's critically important to refrain from having sex before marriage — even though most the world says "Go for it!" Gentlemen, talk about it with your fathers and then be bold enough to be different from your pals. Holding off on sex is a big decision, and easier said than done. But it *can* be done, and it's totally worth it.

Sex is such a powerful force that it can easily skew our thinking about the women we meet. Sex adds a whole new dynamic into any relationship and can mess with our decision-making. A man's intense desire for the sexual bond can make us say and do things we normally wouldn't. Have you ever heard the expression, "A guy is thinking with his penis?" Sad, but true. There are plenty of relationships that are based on pure physical attraction and ignore the more important part of the equation.

Relationships based primarily on sex are only good for an hour or so per week. But you still have to live with that person during the other 167 hours!

Some say you should experiment with multiple partners — sow some wild oats — before committing to just one woman for the rest of your life. I would argue that premarital sex has negative repercussions you can't even imagine, with lasting emotional consequences. That's because sex is probably the most memorable experience a human can have. Anyone you have sex with will be "with you" for your entire life — imprinted in your brain. You will take them with you wherever you go. Forever. Even if you try not to. Trust me, holding off on sex until marriage will be a great gift to your future wife and your relationship.

What are the benefits of waiting to have sex until you're older? What are the risks?

_____

_____

_____

No Tech Relationships

With today's technology, it's tempting to get so absorbed in the cyber world that we almost forget about face-to-face relationships. Social media and video games are fine, but don't allow them to consume your life. It's easy these days to define our relationships through technology, but texting, gaming, and Snapchat are not a good substitute. Relationships require that we interface in person using our words, thoughts, and emotions. Don't hide your feelings behind a screen. Technology makes everything seem so easy and instantaneous, but real flesh-and-blood relationships require hard work.

Learn to enjoy the ups and downs of personal interactions. Appreciate the highs and lows of spontaneous conversations. Enjoy the unpredictability of people. Make sure to take risks in relationships and put yourself out there. The payoffs are huge — and not limited to 280 characters!

My Personal Story #4: Keeping it Real

Many of the friendships I've had in life have been superficial.

But not because I wanted it that way. In fact, I've always desired to have a deep brotherly connection with other guys, but struggled to find and maintain those friendships.

A few years back, I was asked by a friend to attend a "Men's Story Weekend." I agreed to check it out. It was a group of ten adult men who basically spent the entire weekend sharing their life stories with one another. It was one of the most powerful experiences I've ever had. I'd grown up thinking that our failures were meant to be kept private, and only our bright and shiny good stuff should be shared with others.

I was wrong.

I discovered there's power in our stories. I discovered our life experiences shape us, and making some sense out of it all was healthy. But the *best* part of the weekend was having other guys listen to me. They truly, actively listened to me — uninterrupted for an hour. They wanted to know me. Not just the glossy, "everything's perfect" Mike McCormick that I like to project. They wanted to know my core, my essence, what made me tick. This had never happened before. It moved me. It brought up emotions I had locked down my whole life, stuff I had packed away for years that was waiting to get out.

After that experience, I went on more story weekends. A group of my friends formed what we affectionately called the "Man Cave." We gathered together once a week to openly share what was going on in our lives. This was during the height of the 2008 recession and guys were struggling valiantly to hold onto their lives. Some guys had lost their jobs, others lost their marriages, and some had even lost their faith.

Life has it peaks and valleys. We naturally want to stay on the mountaintop as long as we can. It's fun and beautiful up there, but we tend to learn the most down in the valleys — in the desert during our wilderness trials. This was on full display in the Man Cave.

This "band of brothers" came together every week to just listen and support one another during hard times. Guys laid their hearts on the line for each other. And sometimes we had to share tough love with a brother, speak some unvarnished truth, and kick each other in the pants. It was real and raw and beautiful. We were a motley crew. We weren't hanging out together because we were the smartest, richest, or best-looking guys. But our commitment to listening, supporting, and speaking truth to each other created a priceless connection.

The Man Cave has since dispersed, and many of us have scattered to different places across the globe. But to this day, these guys remain some of my best friends, and I know that if I'm ever in need, I can call on my brothers. That's what friendship looks like. It's what all men crave and what all men need in our lives.

Movie to Watch Together: *Shallow Hal*

In the comedy *Shallow Hal*, the main character (played by Jack Black) demands female physical perfection. Then he learns to move beyond superficiality and to appreciate the inner beauty of people . . . including a saintly 300-pound woman.

Discussion Questions:

1. Why was Hal trying so hard to be a "player" at the beginning of the movie?

2. What was Hal's initial attraction to Rosemary based on? How did that change as the movie progressed?

3. Men are very visual; we enjoy beauty. Hal had motivational guru Tony Robbins to help him get beyond physical attraction to see the real person inside. How do we do that?

4. Mauricio said, "Pretty girls don't have to be funny, nice, and smart — but the ugly girls do." Was he right?

5. Could you see yourself kissing somebody like Rosemary? Did you know that "overweight" Rosemary is played by the same actress as "hot" Rosemary? Does that help you think any differently?

6. Why was Hal's neighbor, Jill, all of a sudden interested in Hal after he started dating Rosemary? Do girls really want deep or shallow guys?

7. Tony Robbins said, "The brain sees what the heart wants it to feel." What did he mean ?

8. How did Hal handle the situation in the fast-food place when the guys were making fun of Rosemary? Which of our other Guideposts did he demonstrate?

9. Hal was mad at Mauricio when he was changed back to having a superficial lens. Wouldn't it be cool if we could see beyond people's appearances and really see their inner beauty? What would change?

10. How did Hal's interaction with Cadence at the Burn Unit impact him?

(Jack Black is transformed. *Shallow Hal,* 2001, Twentieth Century Fox. PG-13)

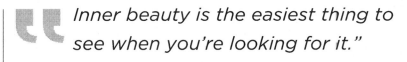

Inner beauty is the easiest thing to see when you're looking for it."

— Tony Robbins (in *Shallow Hal*)

NOTES

_____

_____

_____

_____

_____

_____

_____

_____

_____

_____

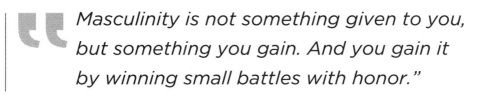

Masculinity is not something given to you, but something you gain. And you gain it by winning small battles with honor."

— Norman Mailer, Amercian novelist

Guidepost 5:
Stay Awake!

| *A man is alert and open to what's happening all around him; always searching for the deeper meaning of life.* |

Eyes Wide Shut

We were all born with hearts full of awe of wonder. When we're young, the world is open and new and exciting. Our imagination and zest for life was limitless. Recently, I watched a two-year old boy as he was walking with his father. He was fascinated with everything he encountered. He picked up some dirt to feel its texture. He jerked his head quickly to watch a bird fly by. He found a stick lying on the ground and put it in his mouth to see what it tasted like. He ran his hand over the blades of green grass and watched them fall back in place. He was awestruck with everything that was happening around him.

Do you remember when life was so captivating?

The older we get, the harder it is to hold onto this sense of wonder. Why? Because life is hard. Pain, fear and struggle dulls our senses and the miracles around us can become mundane. As we focus on completing our daily activities and responsibilities, we forget how to drink in the moment and enjoy life's simple pleasures. But this is precisely where life is meant to be lived!

If you look deep into the eyes of most adult men, there's not much there. No passion, no energy, no impact. We were meant to be a life-giving force in the world, but most guys are sleepwalking through life in a hypnotic trance. Simply going through the motions; trying to squeeze out a little bit of fun here and there is no way to live. If we're really honest, most guys wake up in the morning and don't want to do their day. But it doesn't have to be this way!

When have you ever felt most alive and why? How about *you*, Dad?

_____

_____

_____

The Age of Distraction

There's no doubt about it, life is tough. As men, we're rarely taught how to deal with negative emotions. Instead, we seek comfortable places to run away from our problems. We learn to cope with hardships by finding distractions to give us temporary relief. Often we call them "hobbies" or "pastimes."

What's *your* favorite distraction? Is it food, gambling, social media? Is it golf? How about pornography, music, or fishing? Is it Netflix, Fortnight, fantasy football? Maybe it's fitness or shopping. Maybe it's alcohol or drugs. We tend to use these things to give us a little jolt of energy and spice things up a little.

Our favorite distractions aren't always bad for us, but they're certainly not the best.

The greatest challenge of life (and the sweetest payout) is sharpening our awareness and living honestly in the present moment. The key is learning how to experience the reality of what already is, staying in touch with who we already are and being open to grow in new ways. It's knowing that pain, sorrow, joy, happiness, despair, and boredom are all part of the deal — and choosing not to run from them or to expect anything different.

Unfortunately, we waste many of our waking hours anticipating what will happen in the *future* or dwelling on what has already happened in the *past*; missing the here and now.

Learning to embrace the miracle of the moment is an ongoing, lifelong process. It takes immense openness and allowing a daily quiet space for reflection/prayer, and the courage to peel away the onion and dig a little deeper. It takes mentors, counselors and spiritual advisors to guide us. It takes a fresh set of eyes to see things differently. This is the deeper journey.

Where do you go to find comfort and make yourself feel better? What do you tend to do?

_____

_____

_____

Explore the Unexplainable

An important part of staying awake is being open to the mystery of life and allowing yourself to be surprised every day. Men love easy answers, but many things in life don't have rational explanations. How often do we stand in awe and ask life's deeper questions?

How did creation come into existence and how is it being sustained?

How is it that I know I am here?

Where did my first breath originate?

Where do my joy and suffering come from?

From an early age, men are taught to be logical. Our culture wires us to eliminate anything mysterious, confusing, or outside our comfort zone. We learn if it can't be fully explained, it's not true or reliable. But most of the deep questions of life are unknown and unexplainable. Instead of casting them aside, we need to look deeper. There is something bigger and beyond us.

Faith in a higher power is certainly a choice, but it's not an irrational choice or a blind leap of faith — especially when you look at the mind-blowing complexity and orderliness of our existence. In his book *What We Talk About When We Talk About God*, Rob Bell marvels at the wonders of our earth, the universe, and the human body …

> *"Let's start with our bodies. Each human has around 70-trillion cells, every one of those cells contains hundreds of thousands of molecules with six feet of DNA in every cell containing over three billion letters of coding. That's some incredible craftsmanship to say the least. Think of all of the systems in the human body that have to work together every moment for us to even be living (circulatory, nervous, cardiovascular, digestive, urinary, etc.). Throw in that humans have consciousness (we know we are here) and the miracle of reproduction, and it's pretty awe inspiring."*

How did all of this happen? If that doesn't blow your mind, consider this …

> *"The edge of the universe is roughly 90 billion-trillion miles away. The solar system in which we live in, which fills less than a trillionth of available space, is moving at 558,000 miles per hour. It's part of the Milky Way galaxy and it takes our solar system about 200-250 million years to orbit the Milky Way once. And the universe is always expanding!"*

How did this all materialize and when?

> *"Think of a chair — a tangible, material, physical object. It's actually made up of particles in motion, bouncing off each other, crashing into each other, coming in and out of existence billions of times in billionths of a second. The chair has mass and shape and texture, and can hold you up, yet your chair is ultimately a relationship of energy. Things like chairs and tables and parking lots and planets may appear to be solid, but they are at their core endless frenetic movements of energy. The primary essence of reality is energy."*

Do you ever stop to think about all of the invisible forces at work just to keep our existence in play? It's pretty awe-inspiring! Albert Einstein once said, "There are only two ways to live your life. One is as though nothing is a miracle. The other is as though everything is a miracle."

In your opinion, what is the most mind-blowing part of this world or universe? Could it (or you) exist by chance?

_____

_____

_____

20/20 Vision

Religious teachers throughout the ages have recognized that human beings struggle with poor vision; we rarely see what's truly happening. Religion isn't meant to be a list of rigid rules and regulations or a bunch of "dos and don'ts." Instead, spiritual practices should teach us how to experience the divine, see with greater clarity, and learn to be grateful for our present reality. Spirituality teaches us to drink in the beauty of creation, wonder at our existence, and recognize there is something bigger in our cosmos. Jesus was constantly telling his disciples to "wake up" and truly see the meaning behind the meaning.

There's a deep yearning in all of us to reclaim the childlike wonder we once enjoyed. To see it all anew with a fresh set of eyes. Spiritual disciplines have one main purpose: to expose the illusions in our heads that keep us self-indulged and distracted so we can better see and experience the miracle of the moment.

One of Jesus' most important teachings was that everyone needs to go back to square one and become re-born. To start anew and see with the eyes of a child. But there's no easy way to shed the layers of baggage (fear, pain, skepticism, insecurity) we've accumulated over the years. Regaining the 20/20 vision we once enjoyed in our childhood is a lifelong, spiritual journey.

Richard Rohr says, "Once we allow the entire universe to become alive for us again, we are living in an enchanted world. Nothing is meaningless; nothing can be dismissed. It's all whirling with the same beauty, the same radiance. We can either allow it and let it *flow* through us or we can deny it, which is to deny the divine image." It's never too late!

What can you do to find your childlike wonder again? How about *you*, Dad?

_____

_____

_____

Curious Sponge

As a young man, it's important to discover *what* you believe and *why* you believe it. Most of us are given our belief system at a young age and we never ask the important questions why. We find a safe and happy place and choose to stop learning and growing.

When it comes to life, we need to live with a pattern of discovery as "curious sponges." A curious sponge soaks up new information and experiences in order to learn and grow. He is open to new opinions and perspectives and put his beliefs to the test. He enjoys asking the deep questions and is not content with ready-made answers. The spiritual journey is a gradual path of deeper realization and transformation. It is never a straight line, but a back and forth, up and down, topsy-turvy road. It's the journey of a lifetime!

What can you do to discover, deepen or choose your own faith/beliefs?

_____

_____

_____

My Personal Story #5: The Fog

For most of my life, I've been afraid. Fear has dominated my existence and I've been scared of just about everything in my path. When anything difficult, painful or unplanned comes my way, I have a tendency to go inward and zone out. In fact, my high school basketball coach not so affectionately referred to me as "The Fog." I've always struggled to "stay awake."

I believe much of my fear came from my religious upbringing.

Growing up, I pictured God as some white-haired, bearded dude up in the sky sitting on a throne, looking down, ready to drop some thunderbolts and zap me when I screwed up. I tried my best to do everything I could to stay off God's "naughty list" and keep my nose clean. In my eyes, God was a critical spectator and a cosmic killjoy waiting for me to mess up. However, if I got in a jam (like whenever I needed a good grade or some extra strength for a big game), I'd toss up a few prayers for some help. This was my view of God for the first 22 years of my life.

Since then, I've been doing my best to go back to the beginning. Trying to deal honestly with my pain, to see God with a fresh set of eyes and putting myself out there.

A couple of years ago, the pastor at my church asked me to host a Sunday service while he was on vacation. My job was pretty simple. I needed to welcome everybody, thank the band for the music, and introduce a video message. I would share the announcements and close out the service.

Everything started out fine. I introduced the video message and then sat down to watch it with everybody else. The room darkened. The video came on for about five seconds and then unexpectedly shut off. I waited for a few moments with dread in my heart. I could feel 300 pairs of eyes looking at me. I got out of my seat and slowly sauntered onto the stage praying that the tech team would get it together and save me. No such luck. It wasn't fixable.

For the next 20 minutes, I gave an impromptu sermon on the topic of grace. Don't ask me what I said because I have no idea. It was the perfect topic because I certainly needed people to give me a lot of grace … which they did!

At this point, you may be saying, "If that's what a spiritual journey looks like, I want nothing to do with it." Most people would choose death over spur-of-the-moment public speaking. But here's the thing. Somehow, I *knew* that I was going to have to give a sermon on that day.

At 2 a.m. the night before, I was wakened by a howling wind blowing against my window pane. For whatever reason — call it God or paranoia — I felt like I needed to be ready in case the power went out at church. So I went downstairs and watched the prerecorded video message with a strange feeling in my heart that I might need to personally deliver the sermon.

So when the video didn't work, I wasn't completely surprised. I smiled to myself, shook my head, and walked up to do what I believed would happen. I didn't have to be a pastor or a priest. I didn't have to have a carefully-crafted sermon prepared. I had all I needed.

When you open your heart and mind to the divine presence, things don't automatically become smooth sailing. In fact, you may be pushed beyond your natural human abilities. I've found it to be an adventure full of peaks and valleys and twists and turns that can be black-diamond treacherous. The adventure sports industry rakes in billions as thrill seekers pursue the next new adrenaline rush. But paddling down the Amazon, hang-gliding off the Alps, or trekking the Himalayas can't compare to the excitement of going on a journey with God!

Movie to Watch Together: *The Matrix*

In *The Matrix*, computers have taken over the world and enslaved humans. Artificial intelligence has created a virtual reality so complete that people don't even realize they are imprisoned. Freedom fighters and computer hackers in this dystopian future work to emancipate the human race.

Discussion Questions:

1. Neo (played by Keanu Reeves) says, "I don't believe in fate because I don't like the feeling that I'm not in control." Can you relate to Neo wanting to be in control of his life rather than God?

2. Morpheus (played by Laurence Fishburne) says, "You are a slave, Neo … born into bondage. Into a prison that you cannot taste or see or touch. A prison for your mind." How does this quote relate to the concept of "false self?"

3. Morpheus gives Neo a choice to take the blue pill (live in happy denial) or the red pill (live in the real world). Later, when Cypher dines with Agent Smith, he holds up a piece of steak and says "I know this doesn't exist, but ignorance is bliss." Even though he knows the truth, why does Cypher choose to live inside the Matrix? Do we make similar choices?

4. When Neo was learning kung fu, Morpheus tells him, "I'm trying to free your mind but you're the one who has to jump through it." Any similarities between that statement and how God engages us? Are you jumping or standing still?

5. Cypher makes a deal with the devil (Agent Smith) when he turns Morpheus in. What were his goals for himself once he returned to the Matrix? Do you crave some of the same goals for your life?

6. The last line of the movie has a profound message: "I know you are afraid. You are afraid of change. I didn't come and tell you how it will all end. I came to tell you how it will begin. I came to show these people what you don't want them to see. A world without you. A world without rules and controls. A world where anything is possible. Where we go from here is a choice I leave you." Neo is describing what "life to the full" feels like. How would this look in your life?

(Winner of 4 Academy Awards. *The Matrix*, 1999, Warner Brothers. Rated R.)

> *You are a slave, Neo ... born into bondage. Born into a prison that you cannot smell or taste or touch. A prison for your mind."*
>
> — Morpheus (Played by Laurence Fishburne)

Six Rugged Truths
(Every Man Must Know)

Before *ManQuest* comes to a close, I have to lay some hard truth on you. It's tough love and it may sound negative. But trust me, it's not meant to be a downer, it's meant to be a wake-up call.

In his book, *Adam's Return,* Richard Rohr says, "All great spirituality is about what we do with our pain." In many cultures, a boy's rite of passage still includes pain — getting a slap in the face or some other painful reminder that life isn't just a "bowl of cherries." While we don't wish to inflict physical pain, we want you to know that life is hard and you can't avoid pain (no matter how you try).

A man can waste his entire life playing it safe and trying to hide from the rugged truths. We want you to enter manhood knowing the real deal so you won't just sit on the sidelines, hoping everything will work out perfectly — sorry, but it won't. I organized my Six Rugged Truths around concepts from Rohr's book, then expanded on them for *ManQuest* participants. So buckle up for some hardcore man-wisdom with a heavy dose of reality.

Ready? **No whining — listen up.**

1. Life Is Pain

Men will do anything under the sun to avoid problems and pain. It's our nature to seek comfort as our main goal in life and find the easiest way to achieve it. We will spend way too much time avoiding the tough stuff and protecting our small goals and fragile egos. But when all is said and done, a man must experience pain. No pain, no gain. It's true in weightlifting and in life. It's how we grow. As men, we are a hard-headed group. It takes a lot to make us change — and hardship is often the best driver of transformation.

For some reason, men don't respect anything that comes too easily. Jobs, trophies, women, scholarships — we all know anything worth having is worth fighting for. There's no free lunch, guys. Remember the movie *Princess Bride*? Wesley, the fair-haired hero, said it best when he told his true love that "Life is pain . . . anybody who tells you differently is selling something."

Abraham Lincoln, Michael Jordan, Thomas Edison . . . Every truly great man hit rock bottom prior to success. He transformed that pain into greatness. The man who risks nothing accomplishes nothing. He foolishly believes that pain will never find him. Wrong! You can run and hide, but there's no guarantee of safety anywhere on this planet. You will eventually be wounded. And guys, it hurts twice as much if you're not expecting it.

2. You Will Fail

Much of the focus on today's parenting is about teaching how to succeed in life. There are travel soccer teams for first graders, SAT prep courses for middle-schoolers, and even French lessons for in-utero babies! We groom for success, but spend very little time teaching kids the important lesson of *failure*. And make no mistake about it — you will fail plenty of times.

It doesn't mean you're a loser if you fail, it simply means you're human. Don't get me wrong, doing your best and making an effort in life is huge. And I'm not giving you license to be a slacker. Just don't kid yourself into thinking that you're going to get it all right all of the time. You will never find true happiness unless you start living with your own imperfections.

As American men, we spend tons of time and energy trying to prove our competence in the classroom, the boardroom and the bedroom. From athletics to business to sex, our personal success is the driving force of our identity. We spend our waking hours (and best years) trying to convince others that we have it all together, when that's just plain impossible.

Most men rarely admit they don't have all the answers. Just watch your dad the next time he's lost somewhere (without his Waze app). Will he stop to ask for directions? No way! Gentlemen, we mess up all the time. Admitting our inadequacies and imperfections creates great opportunities for personal growth and better relationships.

We're not perfect, and never will be. So stop pretending and just go for it!

3. You Are Not in Control

Both hands on the wheel. Check your mirrors. Drive defensively. It feels good to be in control, doesn't it? But on the highway and in life, an unexpected crash could be right around the next corner. The control you feel is only an illusion.

There are enough shreds of evidence out there to make us believe we're holding all the cards. On an average ho-hum day, it's easy to feel large and in charge — but the truth is that each of us is only a split second away from physical, emotional or financial disaster. But as humans, we ignore the overwhelming evidence that random events affect us all! Why? Because it's hard to admit we have absolutely nothing to do with most of the major outcomes in our lives.

When we finally face the reality that our range of control is pretty small, we become situated correctly in the universe. There is euphoric joy and release at this point. It's humbling, but it's freeing. When we stop trying so hard to run our own lives, we are more open to the world around us.

4. You Will Get Lost

There will certainly be times when you find yourself helpless and hopeless, flailing away in desperation at something you can't change or even understand. There will be days when you'll ask, "How in the heck did I ever get here? This is not the course I set for my life." You will feel numb and unable to move in any direction. You'll be afraid and angry at the same time. At this moment you'll probably shake your fist at God and demand to know why God isn't helping solve your problem. When the hissy fit is over, you'll probably beat yourself up for not being able to extract yourself out of whatever funk, quagmire, or hot mess you're in.

When you find yourself in this inevitable fog, here's what to do: Be still. Sit with the discomfort and uncertainty. Sit with the fear and anxiety that may come. Then listen. Breathe. Quiet your anxious mind. Notice the fears and emotions that are consuming you, but don't let them control you. The divine presence is with you and in you — and even if the road ahead is dimly lit, you will be guided step by step.

5. It's Not About You

Most self-help gurus will tell you that life is all about you. Grab all the gusto you can, live large, and claw your way to the top. Even some preachers say that health and wealth and happiness should be your all-important goals. The opposite concept ("it's not about me") puzzles a lot of people. Why? Because the prevailing message in our selfish, consumer-driven culture screams, "You deserve the best! Look out for Number One!" Guys, please know that you are not useful to anybody (even yourself) until you grasp the upside-down truth that real wealth consists of what you *give away*, not what you *store up*.

Sure, you can spend life indulging yourself and feeding your ego. Lots of people do. You might be able to earn a comfortable lifestyle, impress your peers, and even convince most people that you're happy. But until you start devoting your time and resources to a cause greater than yourself, you will be missing what matters most — a life of meaning and purpose. If you have no greater cause than the "me monster," you'll feel an emptiness and discontent that will gnaw away at your soul. As Richard Rohr says, the privileges of manhood are given only to those who pay some dues to the common good.

Your success in life has a built-in responsibility to others.

6. You Are Going to Die

Brace yourself — you are not immortal. Everyone who reads this book is going to die. Hopefully not today, or tomorrow, or even 50 years from now, but make no mistake, you will eventually kick the bucket. An old Hindu proverb says, "The surprise of surprises is that although everybody who has ever lived in this world has died, for some reason, each of us thinks we will be the exception."

Thanatophobia is the fear of death. And the people with the greatest fear are those who've never truly lived in the first place. When you haven't experienced the divine presence, the idea of physical death can feel scary, impossible, and unthinkable.

Personally, I'm not in a big hurry to die — and I want to make sure I live life to the fullest before I do!

Final Exhortation

There you have it . . . *ManQuest* laid out for you in black and white. Now, it's up to you how you want to apply it to your life, no matter what age you may be.

If you commit to living by the 5 Guideposts, you'll have a better shot at living life with meaning and purpose. If you choose to exist without a clear and compelling definition of manhood (or buy into our culture's false definition), you're more likely to live with the nagging suspicion that something important is missing. It's your decision. No one can make it for you. But if you do decide to step into this adventure, you're in for a wild ride!

In closing, there are three important messages I want you to remember about *ManQuest*:

1. Being a man is awesome!

2. You have all that it takes to become an amazing man.

3. You can't do it alone. Get help when you need it. Make sure you reach out to your dad or a male mentor during the journey whenever you are stuck or confused.

Enjoy the ride! The journey to manhood is a lifelong experience. You never quite fully "arrive," but the journey is the destination!

Epilogue: Ripples

It was a magical time.

My own son's *ManQuest* experience ended with a weekend initiation ceremony at a beautiful lake in northern Michigan. I was part of a group of fathers who had carefully planned every detail of the spring getaway specifically for our boys. Each activity and experience was designed to create opportunities for the 13-year-olds to cement the lessons they had learned about living as a man.

In the weekend's final exercise, the teens were to spend a couple of hours in quiet seclusion, reflecting on their experience and the journey to manhood (a lofty assignment for any age). Each young man chose a peaceful spot free from distraction. His dad or mentor gave him a personal letter of encouragement and then found a quiet place to wait.

My son, Xavier, chose to spend his time of solitude on a beach just around the bend from the cottages where we were staying. I grabbed a nearby park bench. After about 90 minutes, he stood up and stretched. Rolling up his pants, he waded out into the cold lake. I watched silently as he picked up smooth stones and started skipping them across the water. I quickly flashed back to his days as a toddler, spending endless hours throwing rocks into water. In those early days, chucking stones was our favorite thing to do. I think we abandoned this simple pleasure when superheroes and T-ball took over. But on this day, with plenty of time to relax and reflect, he enjoyed a blast from the past and spent an entire hour tossing rocks into the icy spring waters.

Suddenly, he paused and dropped a single rock into the water. As the ripples spread, I watched him gaze across the smooth surface of the lake. Then out of nowhere — from about 200 yards off shore — the wind and water seemed to conspire and collide, sending a rogue wave rushing towards Xavier in the shape of an arrowhead. Within seconds, the tip of the watery arrow passed right through his legs. As the shimmering wave crashed on the beach, the sun peeked out of the clouds and seemed to shine down upon him. I shook my head in amazement. I had never seen anything like it. It was a one-in-a-million combination of nature's power and beauty, and from where I sat, it seemed to have specifically targeted my son.

I wasn't sure if he had even noticed this strange phenomenon. But I was sure of one thing — he didn't pick up any more stones.

In a few moments, I left my bench to tell him it was time to rejoin the group. Before walking back, we sat down on the beach. I asked if there were any takeaways from his time of solitude. I honestly wasn't expecting any great revelations or huge epiphanies.

And I certainly wasn't expecting to see tears of joy in my son's eyes.

Wiping away the moisture, he told me he had "heard from God." While he was busy throwing rocks, he was pondering whether or not he was ready to be a man. He said he enjoyed being a boy, and while it was nice to learn about manhood, he questioned whether he really wanted to make the journey. As he was struggling with this decision, he decided to drop one final rock into the water and ask God to give him some kind of unmistakable sign to guide him.

Xavier explained that dropping the rock was symbolic of him letting go of childhood pursuits. Excitedly, he recounted that the instant the rock hit the water, an incredible sparkling wave came rolling across the lake, aimed directly at him. As the water rushed past, a school of minnows that had pooled at his feet started kissing his toes. Tearfully, he told me how he had received the answer he needed. We cried and hugged and gave thanks for the incredible sign we had both witnessed.

We lingered on the sand, chatting about his experiences. I shared that while becoming a man is never easy, there's no greater journey to be on. I told him how happy I was that he was well on his way. To his great relief, I assured him that real, authentic men can still have fun in life and still enjoy their childhood pastimes.

By then it was time to rejoin the group. But before leaving this hallowed ground, we made sure we threw a few more rocks and skipped a few more stones.

Note: Five years later, Xavier decided to write his college essay on this experience. To this day, he says it was the most profound experience he's ever had.

NOTES

Appendix A:
Kick-Off Event Agenda

Before starting this epic boys-to-men journey, I suggest holding a "Kick-Off" Ceremony. To help dads get their boys ready for *ManQuest*, they should get out into nature and introduce the concept in a memorable and ceremonial fashion. Here's a sample agenda you can use:

1. Fathers gather sons together in a quiet place.

2. Leader tells the young men that this is serious business and they need to remain quiet and respectful throughout what is about to take place.

3. Each dad will lead his son to a private place and put a bandana blindfold over their eyes.

4. The father will ask for his son's trust and then zip-tie his hands.

5. Dads will read the following script to their son:

"I have brought you here tonight for a very special reason with a very special purpose. Tonight is the first step in your journey to becoming a man. You are here because you are ready to start learning the *ManQuest*. I will be your guide in this process.

"You are shackled and blindfolded because I want you to know what it feels like to be lost and confused. As a man, you will feel lost at times. There are powerful forces in this world that want you to feel lost and hopeless. In these moments of darkness, you will need to put your trust in what you cannot see. During these times you must move forward until you are back in the light.

"I see strength in you! I see greatness in you! You have unique abilities that will take you through the tough times. You have been blessed with qualities like_____ and _____.

"As you become a man, God will expand these gifts . . . and I can't wait to see the great things you will do.

"As you go on this journey to manhood, I want you to know three important things:

    1. Being a man is awesome!

    2. You have what it takes!

    3. I will be right there to guide you along in this process.

"Do you trust me? Good. Now I'm going to put my hand on your shoulder and guide you toward the light. Are you ready to go?"

6. Dads lead young men to the bonfire and stand behind their son.

7. Group leader reads the following script to blindfolded, zip-tied young men:

"I want absolute silence and your full attention because the words I am about to speak are words you have never heard before. They are the words of life that you must know. This is serious business. Before today, you were not ready to hear the secrets of true manhood. You are here today because your father feels you are now ready.

"Fathers and mentors, I ask you, are your sons ready to start the journey to manhood? Are your sons ready to be brought into the inner circle of manhood? If so, say YES. . .

"The first thing you need to know is that as an American male you were born into slavery. Not slavery of the body but slavery of the mind. That's why your hands are bound. Our culture sends you false messages that will keep you weak, confused, and powerless little boys. As your fathers — men who love and care about you — we will not allow this to happen.

"Society has already filled your brain with lies about what it means to be a man. But being rich doesn't make you a man. Getting with lots of women doesn't make you a man. Being a superstar athlete doesn't make you a man. Being a man is much more than these trivial, superficial goals.

"Over the next few months, you will be taught the *ManQuest*. You will learn what it means to be a man. It will not be easy. You will be given 5 Guideposts to learn, understand and apply to your life. You must hold onto these Guideposts when the storms of life try to pull you under. You must write them on your hearts so you don't waver when you are put to the test. "You will prevail!

The Five Guideposts are:

1. Lead Courageously

2. Pretend About Nothing

3. Protect Your Heart

4. Engage in Deep and Meaningful Relationships

5. Stay Awake!

"Take off your blindfolds. You are no longer in the dark.

"Look around you. These are the men who you will journey with. What you hear and say with regard to the *ManQuest* stays among this brotherhood. It is not to be shared with anybody other than this group. The *ManQuest* experience is confidential and sacred.

"In the next couple of weeks, your father will be sharing something very special with you. If he hasn't already done so, he is going to share his life story with you. You need to know him and his story. You need to know his successes and failures in life. You need to learn from him. If you have questions, your father will be your guide.

"Remember these three things you must know about the *ManQuest* process:

1. Being a man is awesome!

2. You have what it takes!

3. Your father will be right there to guide you.

"Congratulations! Your journey has begun."

Appendix B:
Crossover Weekend Agenda

At the end of the *ManQuest* journey, I suggest holding a Grand Finale "Crossover" Weekend. A group of dads and sons should get out into nature (campground, cottage, park, etc.) to avoid distractions and create a powerful final experience.

Can't do a weekend?
If you can't pull away for a weekend, make sure to do a daytrip or an afternoon. It's so important to end well! Regardless of how much time you have available, there are three essential components to the ManQuest finale: 1) an activity, 2) a feast, and 3) the father's blessing. Make sure at the end of the experience every father shares what he admires about his son and gives him his blessing.

The following is a sample agenda you can use:

DAY 1

Noon — 5:00 PM — Arrival

6:00 — 8:00 PM — Dinner

8:00 — 9:00 PM — Boys Activity (quick hike, capture the flag, swim, fire building, etc.)

9:00 — 11:00 PM — Camp Fire Time

    A. Purpose of the Weekend

    B. Things we've learned (5 Guideposts Recap).

    C. Dads sharing personal stories pertaining to 6 Rugged Truths

    D. Young men throw childhood toy or token into fire and share its childhood relevance.

DAY 2

9:00 AM — 10:00 — Breakfast

10:00 — 12:30 PM — Adventure Activity that challenges young men with limited father/mentor involvement (canoeing, hiking, white water rafting, "Outward Bound" style activity, etc.)

1:00 — 2:00 PM — Lunch

2:00 — 4:00 PM — Time of Solitude / Listening to God

Dad/Male Mentor:

    A. Allows young man to pick his own place of quiet

    B. Gives him a letter of encouragement

    C. Leaves young man with Questions to Ponder, a journal for time of quiet and reflection

    D. Talks with the young man about his quiet time

4:00 — 5:00 PM — Celebratory Feast

5:00 — 6:30 PM — Camp Fire Time

    A. Open-ended sharing time with group on what they learned through the entire experience, the weekend, or during their time of solitude

    B. Dad/mentor gives his blessing on the young man by placing hand on his shoulder/head as he sits in front of the group

    C. Shares Three Messages every man needs to hear

        1. Being a man is awesome!

        2. You have what it takes!

        3. I am right beside you to guide you.

    D. Final words of encouragement

8:00 PM — Departure

This is a "sample" agenda for a final weekend, but get creative and do your own thing. For example, we've recently adopted a whole new finale around a 24-hour father-son drum building exercise that's been exciting and meaningful. Remember — rituals, symbols, and ceremony are powerful tokens and will create a lasting memory of the experience.

TIP: At the beginning of *ManQuest*, set a date three months in the future and get it on the calendar with all the men in your group. If you don't set a date early, it won't happen. Trust me. Finishing well is huge!

If boys don't learn, men won't know."

— Douglas Wilson

What's a Man Band? It's a collection of 5 silver icons on a black wristband. It was designed and created by a local jeweler friend, Link Wachler. Each unique icon represents one of the 5 Guideposts and is given to the young man only after he completes that Guidepost. For info on obtaining your Man Band and icons, go to *linkwachlerdesign.com* (or call Link at 248-882-2031).

Made in the USA
Middletown, DE
18 July 2020